GROSSE ÎLE

OTHER PUBLICATIONS BY CARRAIG BOOKS

M. O'Gallagher: Saint Patrick's Quebec, 1824-1834. — The building of a church and of a Parish. — The Irish in Quebec City.
Saint Brigid's Quebec 1856-1981 The Irish look after Their own (care of the orphans and the aged).

J. Mangan, F.S.C.: The Voyage of the Naparima: a journal of 1847. — The tragic tale of an Irish family group in 1847.

M. O'Gallagher: Grosse Ile, Porte d'entrée du Canada, translated by Michèle Bourbeau

Clive Meredith: In All Weathers In All Seasons A Quebec Scrapbook; illus. by Elizabeth Abbott Egan

Jeannette Vekeman Masson: A Grandmother Remembers Grosse Ile, translation by Johanne L. Masse of ''Grand-maman raconte la Grosse Ile.''

Cover design by Diane Emery.

Cover: Grosse Ile — Saint Lawrence River: Watercolour on pencil, by Lord Henry Hugh Manvers PERCY (1817-1877) PAC 13620

Copyright © by Carraig Books 1984.
Dépôt légal: Bibliothèque nationale du Québec and the National Library of Canada, second trimester, 1984.
ISBN 0-9690805-3-0

Marianna O'Gallagher

GROSSE ÎLE

Gateway to Canada
1832-1937

Carraig Books
P.O. Box 8733 Ste-Foy
Québec, G1V 4N6

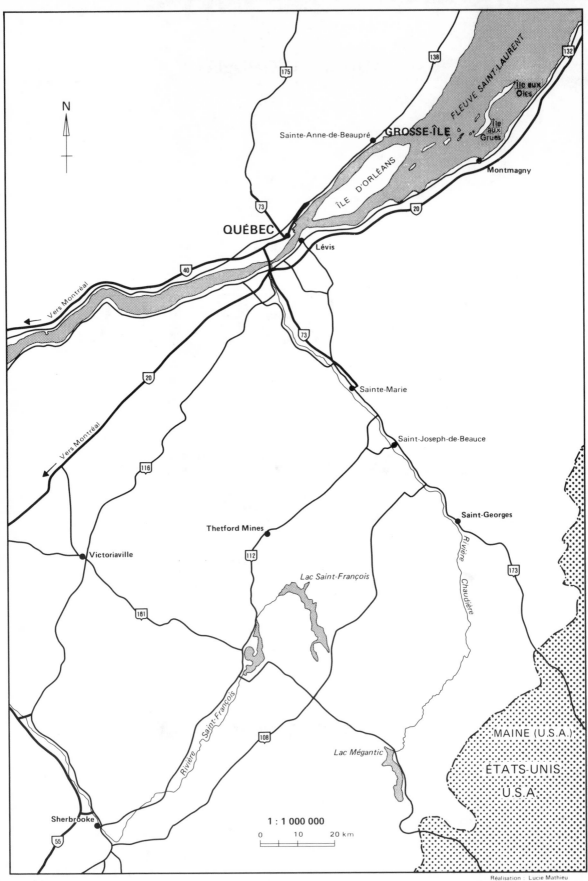

N

138

132

175

FLEUVE SAINT-LAURENT

Île aux
Oies

Sainte-Anne-de-Beaupré   GROSSE-ÎLE

Île
aux
Grues

ÎLE D'ORLÉANS

Montmagny

73

20

QUÉBEC

Lévis

40

Vers Montréal

73

20

Sainte-Marie

Vers Montréal

116

Saint-Joseph-de-Beauce

Saint-Georges

Thetford Mines

173

Rivière Chaudière

112

Lac Saint-François

Victoriaville

161

MAINE (U.S.A.)

ÉTATS-UNIS
U.S.A.

108

Lac Mégantic

Rivière Saint-François

1 : 1 000 000

0   10   20 km

Sherbrooke

55

Réalisation : Lucie Mathieu
Yves Banville
Collège de Limoilou

TABLE OF CONTENTS

PREFACE

Our country, Canada, is the sum of many parts. One of those parts is a past full of those things on which great nations are created. Accomplishments, victories, defeats, individual human suffering, war and compromise, terrible sadness and great joy, great errors and grand successes.

From it all has come a nation which has erased many imperfections of the past in the quest for a just and honorable society. Our continuing quest will be more productive if we know how we got here and the price we paid. In short, we must know our history to build a better future.

This book on Grosse Ile as a human quarantine station helps us know our history. The island with which the author deals is in the St. Lawrence River, an historic waterway on which much of our past was built. In such a location, the island was almost destined to play a significant role in the growth of our nation.

In human terms, Grosse Ile is not always a pretty story. But nation-building is not always a pleasant activity. And Grosse Ile helped build the nation as did all those buried there.

As a quarantine station for European immigrants in the early life of Canada, Grosse Ile was the end of the road, not the beginning, for many seeking a new life in a new land. Many were held on the island for periods of time to prevent the spread of infectious disease into the general population. Many died in quarantine over many years.

When its role as a human quarantine station ended, new activities were found for the historic island. Of great importance in recent history was its use as an Agriculture Canada quarantine station for livestock from Europe. Grosse Ile processed thousands of cattle and other incoming animals to ensure that our livestock population was not decimated by foreign disease. These imports greatly improved our breeding stock in Canada.

Grosse Ile will continue to serve the Canadian people in the future. The quarantine station will remain. But my hope is that the rest of the island with its relics from the past will eventually be turned into a national park. Then all Canadians can visit there to get a better sense of the land they inhabit. It would therefore serve the same commendable purpose as this book.

Ottawa, October 20, 1983   Eugene F. Whelan
                                                         Minister of Agriculture
                                                         for Canada

FOREWORD

It took a long time, about five years of research to bring to light the tragic, yet fascinating story of a little island that looks, from a distance, like a hump on the surface of St. Lawrence River. It is called Grosse Ile. Viewed from Montmagny, on the south bank of the river, it is part of a picturesque landscape with the Laurentian hills rising to majestic Cap Tourmente in the background.

Grosse Ile has passed through a period of almost complete oblivion dating back to the early years of the twentieth century. Fortunately some people in Quebec, people of both Irish and French Canadian descent, did not let the story of the island die out in their memory.

The story of GROSSE ILE, GATEWAY TO CANADA, by Marianna O'Gallagher, makes a substantial contribution towards reminding Canadians of the wealth of meaning contained in the history and the geography of the island.

Marianna O'Gallagher and her blood relatives have always held Grosse Ile dear to their memories. Her grandfather, Jeremiah Gallagher, a distinguished leader in the Quebec community of his day, designed the beautiful monument located on ''Telegraph Hill'' at the west end of the island. Historian, author, archivist, teacher, O'Gallagher is well qualified to tell us the story of Grosse Ile.

The story touches on the Irish immigrant tragedies of 1832 and 1847. In the appendix of the book we find a list of 600 orphans, some of them mere babies, left in the aftermath of the Golgotha that claimed the lives of their parents and guardians.

THE STORY OF GROSSE ILE, GATEWAY TO CANADA is one of several documents being prepared for the 450th anniversary of Jacques Cartier's exploration of the St. Lawrence River.

The climactic point of all the interest being focused on Grosse Ile will be, we sincerely hope, the inclusion of at least the west end of the island under Parks Canada.

James Mangan FSC

INTRODUCTION

This slim volume is a look into the history of an island. It covers the period from 1832 to 1937 — the dates of the opening and the closing of the St. Lawrence Quarantine Station. Between those two dates Grosse Ile established its reputation as an island of sorrow and of mystery. The name Grosse Ile always evokes in Quebec the recollection of "les immigrants irlandais", those of the famine migrations of the late 1840s. But the story and the stories of the island go well beyond that tragic period, and remind us of many other immigrants who came to Canada in those years, and indeed ever since. Never to be forgotten, however, is the fact that the Irish always loom larger than any other national group in the statistical tables at any time in the 19th and early 20th centuries. No wonder, then, that they loom large in the folk memory of Quebec. The treasured belief that French Canadian families adopted orphaned Irish children in 1847 and 1848 is documented here. But the documentation serves another purpose: to show the existence of Irish communities in Quebec and Montreal and elsewhere around the province, whose members also adopted the children of their unfortunate countrymen.

Once Free Trade was adopted by Britain, the Saint Lawrence was open to ships and people from every European nation. Later, both Macdonald and Laurier, as Prime Ministers interested in developing the new country, put emphasis on the welcome of immigrants to Canada. Grosse Ile was there in its capacity of quarantine island, and saw them all: some were obliged to stay on the island for a time, others passed by on the ships that sailed, and later steamed into the harbours of Quebec and Montreal.

The book limns the broad lines of a sketch of Canadian immigration: the reception of thousands of potential citizens from every European nation. On the island, police, nurses and hospital personnel had to be either multilingual, or quick to call for the services of the interpreters whose role often became that of interpreting customs and situations, and not mere words.

The influence of Grosse Ile spread far beyond the valley of the Saint Lawrence. The medical authorities there, members of the Dominion Quarantine Services, exercised vigilant attention, and at times responsible command, over those it deemed were in its care.

When its quarantine role came to an end in 1937, the island was by no means abandoned. During World War II it was used as an experimental station by the Armed Forces: more mystery and secrecy which is only now being breached — but that is beyond the scope of this book. After the war, under the Department of Agriculture, the island sheltered European cattle, imported on the hoof, while they underwent medical tests and the quarantine before being integrated into Canadian herds. The scientists who worked on Grosse Ile after the war have yet to be heralded for their contribution to the health and prosperity of the North American cattle industry.

But all that is material for another book or two.

Thanks are due to a small catalogue of people: archivists are in the forefront of the list: National Archives in Ottawa; in Quebec — the Archives of the diocese of St. Anne de la Pocatière; of the Soeurs de la Charité de Québec; and of the Archdiocese of Quebec; if posthumous thanks are possible — to my father, Dermot I. O'Gallagher, for keeping all the correspondence of the committee that built the monument at Grosse Ile. I owe a debt of thanks to the Jackman Foundation for financial aid, and also to the Sisters of Charity of Halifax for time to do the work. My warmest thanks are for those closest to me: my family for enlightened criticism and pressure to keep going, especially to Brendan and Terry. The lacunae are all mine.

In addition I had help in many forms little and big, from Thérèse Fournier, s.c.q., Sister Flore Pelchat, s.c.q., Dr. Sylvio Leblond, Enid Mallory and Mrs. Frances Douglas, John F.E. Connell; Patricia Kennedy, James Whalen, and Grace Mulligan Campbell of the National Archives; Jean Egan Gagnon of Quebec who helped with information on the A.O.H.; Alice Brophy and Jeanne Martineau Boulet; Abbé Armand Gagné of the Archdiocesan Archives of Quebec; Parks Canada; Agriculture Canada; Canadian Convent Alumnae; Emmaus Community in Ottawa. Freddy Masson and Lucienne of Montmagny often received me into their home. Jeannette Vekeman Masson and her daughter Rose Dompierre supplied me with competition that helped to spur the book forward.

I dedicate this book to helpers. They appear directly in some places in the book; they are quietly present in the background throughout. They are present today at many a turn, those people who deliberately and thought-fully, or simply as part of a job, smooth the rough ways, and make things work. On Grosse Ile, over the more than one hundred years of its history, it was people responding to daily needs in circumstances sometimes extraordinary, sometimes dull, that gave that island its aura of unusual dignity.

As the book goes to press, negotiations are afoot and plans are in the making, to place Grosse Ile in the chain of parks that dot the Canadian landscape with reminders of our history. They are like timevaults into which we can enter for a while to absorb the atmosphere of the past. If it comes to pass that Grosse Ile becomes a park, let it be the place where the visitor is touched for a moment by the drama of immigration and what it meant in the life of each one who came, and also in the life of this vast land of ours.

Quebec City
February, 1984   Marianna O'Gallagher

CHAPTER I

THE SETTING

Grosse Ile is a small island in the Saint Lawrence River about thirty miles downstream from Quebec City. In 1832, it became the focus of administrative attention as attempts were made to prevent the entry of a cholera epidemic into North America. Grosse Ile had been chosen as the station that would provide a place for the inspection of ships coming up the river, and a quarantine for any cholera victims, and thus, it was hoped, keep the dread disease out of the colony. It was chosen because of its location in the river below Quebec City and its position in the middle of the channels that carried the summer fleets of sailing vessels full of immigrants. Today the isle is clothed with a sense of mystery and tragedy as popular imagination keeps alive the memory of many of the events that occurred there.

Grosse Ile is a pretty little island. A British document of 1832 calls it a desert island, but paintings of the time indicate wooded areas. Indeed, its owner kept specific rights to all the timber on the island even during the early period of its rental by the government as a quarantine station, and the workers cut down some of that timber to make way for the building of the hospital sheds and the administration buildings destined for quarantine use. Today, the island is covered with maple and oak and birch; pine and other evergreens, as well as luxuriant bushes: raspberry, blackberry, sumac and wild roses. Poison ivy too gleams through the shrubbery. It is the habitat yet of migrating wildfowl as it was from earliest times. In the 18th century it had evidently become popular among hunters for the Intendant Hocquart in 1731 forbade hunting in the islands without the permission of the Seigneur.

The island, not being inhabited in the 18th century was variously identified in the many documents dealing with its frequent change of ownership. Sometimes the several islands in the archipelago were grouped, but always recognizable. Eventually the name Grosse Ile came to mean that island whereof we speak. Why "grosse" (big) when it is not by any means the largest of the islands in its neighborhood? This has been explained thus: there were two islands called "Ile aux Oies", one "la Petite Ile aux Oies" and the other "la Grosse Ile aux Oies". Hence "Grosse Ile". A map attributed to Fonville about 1699 gives the name Grosse Ile to the island. Another map, without any doubt made by Gédéon de Catalogne, probably around 1709 clearly indicates Grosse Ile. Another during the time of Chevalier de Lévis, 1758, uses the title "Grosse Ile". Certainly the island, in comparison to its immediate neighbours is not large enough to merit the word "grosse". Grosse Ile is just one mile long and half a mile wide, smaller than the nearby Ile aux Grues and Ile aux Coudres, and the very large and lovely Isle of Orleans upstream. Here, where the Saint Lawrence is about ten miles wide, Grosse Ile lies amidst an anchorage somewhat sheltered by smaller islands. The beaches on its approachable southern side, opposite Montmagny, form a sort of stage facing the old river channel — a stage indeed where dire scenes in the drama of Canadian history took place.

This great river, the Saint Lawrence, leads into the heart of North America. In the earliest days of European exploration, the challenge of its size and its mystery were met by the small vessels of the French explorers. Cartier explored it for seven years from 1534 on and failed to make a permanent establishment, but the Saint Lawrence continued as a French fishing ground. Champlain explored it from his Nova Scotia base in the early 1600s, and in 1608 established the fur trading post that became the city of Quebec. Champlain's dream of a great agricultural community on the banks of the Saint Lawrence hardly materialized in his lifetime. He had to be content with his city as a fur trading capital with only signs of an eventual agricultural settlement around it. However, all during the ensuing century and a half of the French Regime, tiny ships brought, in a steady trickle, the thousand settlers who formed the basis of the six million and more French Canadians of today. Besides being an avenue for the entry of settlers, the river, unfortunately, also became the roadway of wars. In the eighteenth century, with the last of those wars between the French and the English, the river changed hands. Its vocation changed too, as it began to carry the raw materials of forest and farm to Europe.

ST. LAWRENCE RIVER TRAFFIC

When the nineteenth century began, Quebec City stood at the head of deep water navigation on the Saint Lawrence. The largest sailing vessels of the day could sail easily only as far as Quebec. Above Quebec, the river was too shallow and narrow to accommodate their draft and their need for space to maneuver in the wind. Thus, Quebec City became an important center of maritime trade, exchange and storage. Ocean vessels transferred their cargo to river craft there, or landed it for storage. The ships then onloaded the raw materials of the colonies' maturing export trade.

The transition from fur as the staple of trade to timber and wheat as the principal economic base was a gradual process. However, at the end of the eighteenth century, the nascent timber trade received a major impetus from the Napoleonic Wars. The French blockade of the Baltic Sea during the course of those wars had effectively cut off Britain's traditional source

16

of the timber required for rebuilding and repairing the ships of the British Navy. The North American colonies benefited from Britain's need. The timber-based economies of New Brunswick, of both Upper and Lower Canada grew apace following the boost experienced in the early 1800s.

Of all the regions in the colonies, Quebec City seemed to draw the greatest profit. It became the focus of all the up-river timber cutting. Timber from the Ottawa River and the other tributaries was floated in huge rafts down the Saint Lawrence and into the coves above and across from Quebec. In addition to the value of the wood in each raft itself, could be added the incidental produce that the rafts carried: barrels of potash and pearl ash; barrels of wheat, and later, of flour.

Such a growth in industry had, of course, been accompanied by the installation at Quebec City of the necessary infrastructures for the efficient conduct of business and commerce. A Board of Trade, through the intermediary of many newspapers, kept the businessmen of the city supplied with information on British economy, on U.S. economy, and on the economy of the neighbouring Maritime colonies. Bankers, brokers, auctioneers, insurance companies had their place in the city. The offices of the English timber firms and of shipping lines, both imperial and colonial dominated St. Peter Street and other waterfront locations.

Ship movement on the river was regulated by Trinity House, the pilots' association. In addition to training and providing pilots to guide the ships on the river during the navigation season, Trinity House saw to other aids to navigation, the laying of buoys when the ice was gone, the manning of light houses, and the publication of regulations regarding landing of passengers and cargo in case of health emergencies.

After the Napoleonic Wars, there was a significant change in shipping. More and more immigrants began to arrive in Quebec on the incoming timber ships. Postwar unemployment in the British Isles, the demobilization of armies, the slowdown and cessation of war industry, plus the continuing clearances of small farms to make way for sheep-raising all contributed to a wave of emigration to the New World. The timber ships were ready to carry emigrants. Shipmasters eagerly converted their hulls outgoing from the British Isles into a semblance of passenger carriers and took on board anyone willing to pay for a trip to America. Thus was born the "emigrant trade" which characterized a great part of nineteenth century shipping betweeen the British Isles and Quebec. This "paying ballast" walked on board, and without too much trouble on the part of the masters, might walk off at Quebec.

For shipowners this solved the problem of returning ships crossing the ocean one way almost empty. Paying passengers supplemented whatever small cargo the ill-fitted ships carried. For British landlords in Scotland and Ireland, the gradual removal of "surplus population" or "sources of unrest" proved a boon. There came about a growing encouragement of emigration as a solution to their problems. Emigration to the colonies was accepted as an integral part of the economic picture. Quebec City was the destination of the timber ships, and thus Quebec City became the destination of the emigrants.

The city adapted to its role: before the navigation season opened in early May and the first Atlantic vessels arrived, the timber offices on Saint Peter Street, and the stevedores in the coves made ready; scores of boarding houses and inns and taverns prepared to receive the throngs of people who would come ashore. Carters on land, and bateaux on the river readied for the task of transporting emigrants and manufactured goods up the river to Montreal and beyond.[1]

THE QUEBEC EMIGRANT SOCIETY

Quite apart from the business structure of the city there was a network of benevolent societies that cared for the immigrants as they landed and went through the city every summer. Prominent among these was the Quebec Emigrant Society.

The Quebec Emigrant Society had been founded in 1818 to look after the throngs of immigrants who landed, in increasing numbers, every summer on the docks of Quebec. The Society provided assistance of many kinds: advice and information; shelter and food, certainly, but its principal role seems to have been to assist the immigrant with passage to the interior, up-river to Montreal and beyond. In the years of its operation from 1818 on, the Society thus acquired experience as well as data and impressions on immigration and on emigrants. It represented a cross section of the city's English population. Religious and political, business and professional people belonged to it.

Equally concerned about immigration, as one might expect, were the medical men of the city. A special hospital, the Marine and Emigrant Hospital had been built to supplement, especially during the summer months, the care offered by the two older hospitals of the city, the Hotel Dieu and the Hôpital Général. During the summer, there were also temporary clinics opened near the piers to tend to the immediate needs of the travelers. The doctors, both French and English from all these hospitals, formed the Quebec Medical Board. When need arose, as during an epidemic, the Medical Board summoned a Health Board drawn from a larger representation of the city: representatives of the wards of the city, plus city administrators and clergymen. The role of the board members was to help to create health and sanitation regulations, then aid in publishing them and enforcing them.

CITY GOVERNMENT

Around the time of the first cholera epidemic, Quebec City was not yet incorporated, hence did not have the form of government that a city

---

[1] Steamships of John Molson, John Goudie and later John Ryan operated in the Saint Lawrence between Quebec and Montreal, and some as early as 1809.

usually has, i.e., a mayor and aldermen elected by the citizens. In 1832, Quebec was just about to receive its Act of Incorporation, but was still being ruled by Magistrates. This system dated back to the time of Murray's conciliar government. One of Murray's first acts, after setting up his council and a system of courts was to name Justices of the Peace who would regulate public order and other matters in both Montreal and Quebec. The Justices were directly under the Assembly in the years before municipal governments were established. The Justices looked after commerce and markets, building of streets, reservoirs, jails; they were responsible for drainage, beaches, sanitation. Hence they received sums of money to tend to these affairs, and were assisted by constables in any police matters.

The justices rotated in office and were assisted by the constables who were elected at given times. In the beginning, all the Justices were English Protestant, since all officials were required to take the test oath before assuming office. After the Quebec Act in 1774, the body of Justices became more representative as Catholics were able to take minor offices with a modified oath. Since the City did have a great many English-speaking people, there was always a preponderance of English-speaking men among the Justices. Notices of regulations were published in the bilingual Quebec Gazette of John Neilson. There were "bellmen" or town criers who gave the news too. The citizens were accustomed to contest regulations, or to protest what displeased them. This was especially true in the relations between the city folk and the military. Quebec was a fortress, hence the military controlled the comings and goings of all through the gates of the city. Incidentally these gates were locked at night — even in the 1830s, until commercial protest brought about a change. There was thus, in the city, a good network for the dissemination of news.

THE CHOLERA EPIDEMIC

THE THREAT OF CHOLERA

About 1826, an outbreak of Asiatic cholera occurred in India. By 1831, it had reached Moscow and thence it spread rapidly across Europe. Quebec newspapers reported its progress into Germany and France and, at the end of 1831, acknowledged its inevitable appearance in the British Isles.

Alert to the obvious connection between the coming wave of immigration and the possible outbreak of cholera in Quebec City, the Quebec Emigrant Society broached the idea of limiting immigration or of proscribing it entirely. Realizing that neither prevention nor limitation of immigration was within their competence, the Society undertook to remind the Imperial authorities, in a formal letter, of the existing Passenger Acts and urged their strict enforcement. Signed by several Quebec businessmen, led by J. Kerr, the President, the "Memorial and Petition" was addressed to Lord Goderich of the Colonial Office and reflected the experience and the knowledge of the Society.[2] The letter reported that the immigration of the preceding year, 1831, had brought 60 000 people into a city whose population was barely 33 000. This meant extreme hardships for all concerned, immigrants and city people certainly, but it also put a burden of impossible responsibility on the members of the Society who took their obligations seriously. The petition asked Lord Goderich to bring the situation to the attention of the Imperial Parliament.

In reminding the Government that the Passenger Acts were supposed to "provide for the health, comfort and subsistence" of passengers, the Society made suggestions. The ship inspection called for in the Acts should be performed at the end of the voyage as well as at its start, said the petitioners, so that infringements might be detected, offending Masters fined, and the abuses removed. In addition to that urgent appeal by the Quebec Emigrant Society to the Imperial Parliament, there was also a letter sent by the Magistrates of the city, led by Thomas Ainslie Young, to the House of Assembly, urging the enforcement of quarantine laws of the colony and requesting authority and funds to protect the city.

THE SELECTION OF GROSSE ILE

The response came from the local colonial government early in 1832 when funds were made available for the care of immigrants:

Assembly of Lower Canada
25 February 1832

An Act to create a fund for defraying the expense of providing medical assistance for sick emigrants and of enabling indigent persons of that description to proceed to their place of destination.

The same day, the Assembly further enacted that a quarantine station should be set up, thus creating a new line of defence against disease.

Assembly of Lower Canada
25 February 1832

An Act to establish Boards of Health within the Province and to enforce an effectual system of Quarantine. Whereas His Excellency the Right Honourable Matthew Lord Aylmer Knight Commander of the Most Honourable Military Order of the Bath, Governor in Chief, hath by a Message bearing date the third day of February one Thousand Eight Hundred and Thirty Two been pleased to recommend that Legislative provision should be made for preventing the introduction of the disease called Asiatic Cholera into this province, and for averting or diminishing the evils which might arise from the introduction thereof, and it is expedient that provision should be made for carrying the said recommendation into effect. May it therefore please your Majesty that it may

---

[2] The signers were Quebec City businessmen: President J. Kerr; Vice-President L.H. Ferrier; Andrew W. Cochrane, Robert Symes, William Lyons, James Harkness, John Cannon, George Keys, George Mountain, J. Charlton Fisher, James George and Charles A. Holt.

be enacted by the King's most excellent Majesty by and with the consent of the Legislative Council and Assembly of the Province of Lower Canada. And be it further enacted by the authority aforesaid that there shall be a Quarantine Ground or Anchorage in the Port of Quebec and that the same shall be as near as may be to Grosse Ile ... marked by buoys, to be laid down under the direction of the Supervisor of Pilots, and every vessel subjected to the performance of Quarantine shall perform the same at anchor at such Quarantine Ground.[3]

From that Act of the Assembly of Lower Canada, there came into existence the quarantine station at Grosse Ile. Arrangements for obtaining Grosse Ile for conversion into a quarantine island were made by the Imperial Government. That government rented the island from its owner, Notary Bernier of Château Richer, a town on the north shore of the river.[4] Actual choice of the site had been made by Captain (later Admiral) H.W. Bayfield,[5] who was then in the process of a survey of the Saint Lawrence that he had begun in 1827. The House of Assembly recorded the choice of Grosse Ile, and viewed the maps of the anchorage (drawn by Midshipman A.F. Bowen, R.N.)

... an anchorage between Grosse Island and Margaret Island.

The harbour was described as being

Three miles in extent between the two islands, 400 to 600 yards wide, 7 to 19 fathoms deep with a good clay bottom. One hundred to one hundred fifty sail, could, we apprehend, lie easily in it.

There followed a list of the regulations to be obeyed by all ships approaching Grosse Ile. They were obliged to stop for inspection at the place marked by buoys. If any one on board had been in contact with contagion, the river pilots had to bring the ships to anchor, with ''a blue flag flying at the fore top-gallant masthead.'' All vessels had to have a certificate of health before sailing the last thirty miles up-river to Quebec City. Once at Quebec, the ships were to undergo yet another inspection by an official who would take note of the certificate given at Grosse Ile, again examine the passengers before allowing the red flag of clearance to be flown. After landing their passengers, the ships then proceeded a little further up-river to the coves for timber loading: Diamond Harbour, Sillery Cove, Sharples Cove and beyond.

The Quebec Mercury reported that as of May 1, 1832, Captain Ralph Alderson and his troops of the 32nd Regiment had gone down to Grosse Ile with Dr. Griffin to set up the station. With them went teams of workmen

---

[3] PAC 202 44/30.

[4] An intensive search of notarial records is being made by the Quebec Gov't.

[5] Captain Bayfield was sent in 1827 to do a survey of the Saint Lawrence. He was accompanied by Lt. P.E. Collins at that time. 30 May 1827, Goderich to Dalhousie (RAPC 1931). The survey eventually resulted in an Atlas of the St. Lawrence. Bayfield donated 53 mineral specimens from the Gulf of St. Lawrence to the Museum of the Quebec Literary and Historical Society (Quebec Mercury, 8 May 1831).

to build the needed quarters. The arrival of the soldiers on the island was the first inkling that Pierre Duplain, the resident farmer, had of the fact that the island was changing hands. He later sued the government for the sudden unnotified intrusion, and the case was not settled until 1834.

The Quebec Gazette treated the setting up of the station with frivolity, it might be said, especially in light of the tragedies that were to occur on the island. "A pretty place," the paper declared, "if dejection is a cause of catching the cholera, we think those stationed on the island may find means to dissipate it."

The soldiers appropriated Duplain's house for themselves. A bakery was built in short order, then the workers put up houses for the doctors and nurses, and the long narrow "sheds" (so-called from the beginning) with their tiers of bunks to receive the sick.

A cannon was installed overlooking the river passage to warn defiant ships that they must stop. (Whether it was ever fired for this is not recorded.) A signal system from the top of Telegraph Hill, the highest part of the island, was put up, visible from St. François de Montmagny, with overland relays to the Citadel of Quebec.

CITY PREPARATIONS

At the same time as these preparations were being made by the civic and imperial powers, the local medical men of Quebec City were active. In November of 1831, the Quebec Medical Board met and elected its officers. Dr. James W. Douglas was chosen to lead in the preparations to fend off the impending epidemic. Dr. Douglas had had experience in India where cholera was endemic. His opinion was that cholera could be carried across the ocean, hence the colony must be prepared. He was opposed in that opinion by some doctors on the board. In spite of that difference of opinion, however, preparations continued. Dr. Tessier, a member of the Medical Board was sent to New York to study methods of preventing the spread of the disease.

Despite the optimism expressed in some quarters that cholera would not cross the ocean, the church wardens of Notre Dame de Québec, with grim realism, purchased land[6] for a cemetery outside the city limits.

Meanwhile, the newspapers, throughout the winter of 1831-32, kept up a stream of articles about cholera. They reported the controversies and the warnings, the facts and the fiction, in almost glib fashion.

THE OUTBREAK OF CHOLERA

The Quebec Mercury treated its readers to a full report of the November 1831 meeting of the Medical Board and to several articles about cholera. One, over the signature of Henry Halford, President of the Quebec Medical

---

[6] The land, purchased from John Anderson, later became the corner lot of de Salaberry Avenue and Grande Allée. Saint Brigid's Home and Saint Patrick's Church and school occupied the site.

Board, ended with the statement: "No specific remedy has yet been ascertained." It reads thus:

CHOLERA

Symptoms: giddiness, sick stomach, nervous agitation, intermittent, slow or small pulse, cramps beginning at the tips of the fingers and toes, and rapidly approaching the trunk giving the first warning. Vomiting or purging comes on; the features become sharp and contracted, the eye sinks, the look is expressive of terror and wildness; the lips, face, neck, hands and feet, and soon after, the thighs, arms and whole surface assume a leaden blue purple or black and deep brown tint, according to the complexion of the individual ... The fingers and toes are reduced in size, skin wrinkled, shrivelled; nails pearly white; larger veins are marked by flat lines of darker black; pulse becomes small or extinct ... The skin is deadly cold; the tongue moist and white ... voice is nearly gone; respiration quick and imperfectly performed ... There are spasms in legs, thighs and loins. Secretion of urine is totally suspended, much vomiting and purging follows. Keep the patient warm, rub with blankets and camphorated spirits, poultices of mustard and linseed in equal parts to the stomach; to legs and feet for warmth. White wine whey, with spice, hot brandy and water or sal volatile in hot water; peppermint cloves. In severe cases 20 to 40 drops of laudanum in the warm drink may be given ... But no specific remedy has yet been ascertained. We await further word from India where more success from bleeding, emetics, calomel, opium may help. (Quebec Mercury, January 14, 1832).

The paper, which all through 1831 had published reports of the deadly progress of cholera through the world assured its readers that the editor did not want to be morbid or alarmist, but that they should be prepared — distance was no safeguard. Accompanying the graphic details from the Medical Board was a curious pseudo-comic letter signed Cholera Morbus who described himself as a lover of dirt, darkness, drunkenness; loving the lazy, dirty, quarrelsome, gluttonous, those enfeebled by debauchery, those enfeebled by quack medicines.

narrow courts, cellars, chambers with unopened windows, in the neighbourhood of gasometers, ponds in the purlieus of public houses, redolent of bad beer, among the effluvia of punch, whiskey and blue ruin.

If a man rises early, opens his windows, white-washes his house often, takes his meals with his family and keeps himself in good humour with his neighbours — I pass by his cheerful hearth to revel in the liver of the drunkard — to sin about the boiling bile of the sulky, the discontented and the litigious. (Quebec Mercury, January 14, 1832).

By the springtime of 1832, however, the tone of the newspaper was less flighty, as the city readied for the opening of navigation and what that season might bring on the ships that were leaving the British Isles in March and April. The ships leaving Liverpool and other ports of the British Isles were crowded: between a hundred and two hundred passengers were usually reported, and this exclusive of children. A voyage lasting from 36 to 80 days could be expected.

In Quebec, readers of the Mercury followed the progress of the cholera. In April it had been reported in the Barbados. There were rumours of outbreaks in Maine, and even in Upper Canada in May. On May 3rd, two vessels ignored Grosse Ile and proceeded up-river to Quebec where they were turned back. These were the Intrepid which had left Hull (England) on March 25, and the Canada which had left Greenock (Scotland) on March 28. On May 10, there were ships reported at Grosse Ile, but no sickness aboard; by May 22, there were 12 ships; between May 26 and June 2, the doctors at Grosse Ile reported that they had already seen 15 101 immigrants. By June 5, the Quebec papers reported that 397 vessels had already arrived at Quebec, compared to the 372 of the previous year.

The summer had begun with more than the usual heavy immigrant traffic, but up to this time (June 5), there were only rumours, no confirmed reports of cholera. A May 26 paper reported that there had been 32 deaths at sea among the immigrants on board the Hebron from Dublin. "They are not supposed to have been from Cholera. She passed exam at Grosse Ile and at Quebec, and there was then no sickness on board."

Meanwhile at Grosse Ile, the doctors were plagued by overwork and by the uncertainty of their own diagnosis of cholera which none of them had ever seen. This pressure led to a series of resignations, or a rotation at the post of Health Officer. Dr. Griffin resigned and went to work in the hospitals. He was replaced by Dr. Fortier of St. Michel. The work was already reaching an enormous extent and not a sign of the dread cholera yet. Before the summer was out, Dr. Tessier and Dr. Crawford had taken their turn at administration.

Not everyone appreciated the work that was going on at the quarantine: that doctors and soldiers and nurses there were trying to stave off a fierce and dangerous epidemic. The newspapers carried daily denials of the presence of cholera, and in addition aired the complaints of passengers about delays at Grosse Ile, and the objections of merchants that their invoices, letters and packages were delayed too.

Finally, when cholera did appear, it was not at Grosse Ile but at Quebec. The ship Carricks from Dublin has traditionally been cited as the carrier, but the following excerpts do not definitively put the blame there. On June 5, the Mercury column "Shipping Intelligence" had carried this entry:

> Captain Park of the Astrea spoke the Carricks, Hudson, from Dublin,
> at Grosse Ile Saturday. The Carricks lost 42 passengers, her carpenter
> and one boy on the passage. From some unknown disease. The remainder
> of the passengers are now in good health.

All the passengers from the Carricks were landed at Grosse Ile, were inspected, released and allowed to reboard and proceed to Quebec. The phrase "from some unknown disease" appears to have put the blame on that ship.

The June 9 Mercury carried Dr. Joseph Morrin's statement that deaths at the Marine and Emigrant Hospital in Quebec City had been from ordinary fever. "Small pox is spreading among the people of the city because these have not been stopped at Grosse Ile ..."

Ironically, in the Mercury's column next to the denial that there had been death from cholera in the city, stood the grim title:

CHOLERA

It is our painful duty to apprise the public that this disorder has actually appeared in the city. Since yesterday morning eight cases have occurred which by eleven of the faculty are declared to have all the symptoms of Spasmodic Cholera. Three deaths have occurred previous to noon this day and there were two others whose lives were despaired of. The disease first appeared in a boarding house of Champlain Street kept by a person named Roach. The patients are emigrants and are said to be some of those who were relanded on Thursday from the Steam Boat Voyageur. One Canadian has been seized with the disorder, he had been working on board a ship, and a woman is said to have been attacked by it at Cap Blanc.

* * *

Three o'clock; We have just heard from undoubted authority that fifteen cases of Cholera have appeared since yesterday and seven have terminated fatally. (Mercury, June 9, 1832).

At Grosse Ile people, in an endless line, were being brought into the unfinished hospitals for shelter and care. Ships anchored. Small boats went out with medical inspectors and returned with sick passengers and their baggage. If the vessels needed cleansing, all passengers had to come ashore.

So sudden and so great was the onslaught of the disease that the island was soon over-crowded with sick, dying and dead. And the ships in their summer procession kept coming. Despairingly the authorities gave up their attempts to stop every ship at Grosse Ile and, with a minimum of inspection and segregation, permitted all but Irish ships to proceed up-river. Previously, the healthy and the sick had been dumped together on the island, thence the healthy and the supposedly recovered were again crowded into the Saint Lawrence River steamboats for passage to the interior. However, before the end of June, ships passed Grosse Ile without being stopped for inspection. By the middle of June, in fact, 25 000 people had landed in Quebec City. The city tried to shelter the overflow from the docks in tents on the Plains of Abraham outside the city walls. The old graveyard inside the city received the corpses of both citizen and immigrant alike, while the new graveyard outside the city limits, near the Plains, served to inter still more, both resident and traveler.

Weekly reports of death grew from 150 to 400 to 475 to 500 ... In August, as many as 600 died between 8 A.M. of the 15th and 8 A.M. of the 16th. The obituary column listed but a few names, usually of prominent citizens ''dead of the prevailing disease.''

All sanatary (sic) regulations failed to arrest the progress of this extraordinary disease though the utmost caution was observed. By summer's end 51, 422 emigrants had entered the colony, but few were detained at Grosse Ile. (Sir John Dorratt, M.D. Quebec B.P.P. 1838).

With the trek of the immigrants up-river went the disease, the terror and the death. Montreal and the countryside surrounding it — 1,000 dead by July 3; Kingston, Toronto, Hamilton, Detroit, Buffalo suffered the same way. On the riverside, between Kingston and Cornwall, the crews of the Durham boats tied up their vessels and fled, refusing to carry the immigrants. Around Quebec City, in the Coves, the raftsmen, newly arrived from the woods appeared to be particularly vulnerable, but there were deaths everywhere in the city. At Beauport, at Château Richer, in the hinterland of Valcartier; down-river at Rivière Ouelle, at Kamouraska on the south shore; up the Richelieu River as far as Lake Champlain, the specter of death strode about...

On Grosse Ile itself, despite the fact that some ships went up to Quebec without stopping, the volume of work did not diminish. Doctors and priests fell sick and died along with their patients. Throughout the summer the ships kept on coming. By September 30, the newspapers reported the "official burials" at Quebec City at 3 292. More than that had died at Grosse Ile.

Finally, in November, the medical authorities announced that "cholera is not at epidemic proportions".

Thus closed in 1832 the first act in Grosse Ile's role as a quarantine station. The island, and the nation too, would have a deal more to experience and to learn as thousands from Europe continued to cross the ocean in search of new homes and new lives in the valley of the Saint Lawrence and beyond.

Grosse Ile had had its baptism of fire. The first testing of the quarantine facility was not its most strenuous, for yet another fearful period was to occur with the famine migration of 1847. Between these two extreme points, the station was able to carry on its work with success.

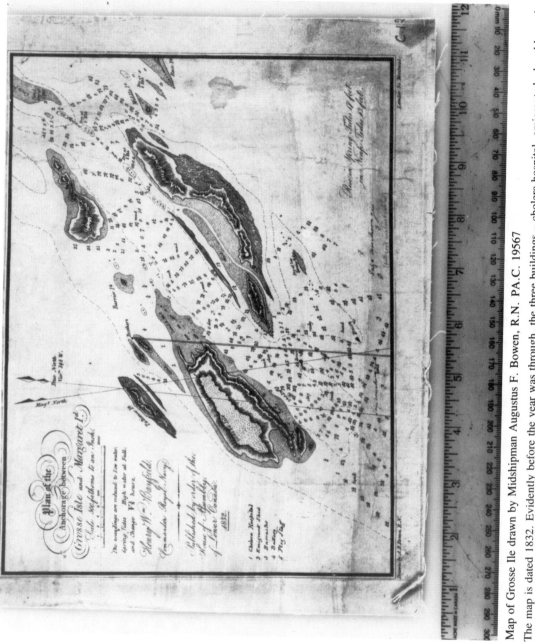

Map of Grosse Ile drawn by Midshipman Augustus F. Bowen, R.N. PA.C. 19567

The map is dated 1832. Evidently before the year was through, the three buildings – cholera hospital, emigrant shed and barracks had been built. Bowen notes the battery and the flagstaff.

P.A.C. 13621 shows the telegraph station. Messages by semaphore were sent to St. François (on clear days) thence to the Citadel at Quebec through other relay stations. The goat is not an accidental or incidental addition. The soldiers kept sheep and goats to augment their rations.

P. A. C. 13630 is identified as "the eatsern end of Grosse Ile". The structure on the beach might be a barge such as were used to transfer passengers from the ships in the stream to the island.

P.A.C. 13624 – an unidentified house about the same period, 1838-39. Once the island station was started, an initial expenditure produced the clearings and the buildings that Percy painted in these illustrations.

P.A.C. 13623 Note the huge stumps. In times of quiet when the station was not being used for guarantine, it was a place for picnics and recreation. The Quebec garrison's officers especially, were able to take advantage of it. Colonel Percy evidently enjoyed several hours, or days of leisure there.

P.A.C. 1228   Captain (afterwards Admiral) Henry Wolsey Bayfield, R.N., did the hydrographic surveys of the Saint Lawrence between 1827 and 1834, published later in London. Bayfield was a member of the Quebec Literary and Historical Association, like many of the army and navy officers of the time, enjoying what Quebec society had to offer.

P.A.C. 46789 Photo by D.A. McLaughlin.
The battery was intended originally to discourage ships from disobeying the injunction to stand in the stream for inspection. The absence of the monument atop Telegraph Hill in the background seems to date the picture before 1909. The substantial buildings range from the pier (the upper pier — le quai d'en haut) inland towards the administration quarter of the island. (Public Works Department)

Casualties in the Shield 1834

Date	Name	Age	Ship	Remarks
May 21st	Died in Hospital the Infant of a woman named Hitchcock separating from			
" 25th	Patrick Honey aged 8 months from Brig Pénélope			Died in Shell of Debility
June 6th	Mimus [illegible]	an adult		
July 21st	[illegible]	2 adult	" "	Accidentally drowned bathing
3rd	Sarah Wightman a child		Bark Celia Crichton	Died in the Shell of Debility
9th	John Hotham an infant		Ship W. Hotham	Landed in a dying state
14th	Patrick Drennan		Bark Ollie	Of Cholera on its road to Hospital by debility after landing its mother "
10th	Geo. Denton aged 40 years		Ship Nelson	Of debility from age
9th	Mary Boab son		Ship Wm Hotham	Premature labour and Cholera
19th	Nell Bonfacy 6		Brig Ed Chitlin	Found dead all-day light is brought
24th	Wm Curtois an infant		"	Died on its way to Hospital from Cholera
24th	John Priater aged 2 years		"	Of Convulsions in the night
" 29th	Chad Hamilton 2		" Mary Cummings	Accidentally drowned bathing
July 29th	Wm Hamilton 20		" "	

Chas Poole M.D.

Med. Supt.

CHAPTER II

THE ROUTINE OF THE STATION

The extraordinary first year of Grosse Ile as a quarantine station was followed by the relatively peaceful summer of 1833. Military and medical authorities tried to carry out the works that ideally should have been accomplished before the station opened.

The island was under the command of a military officer from the garrison at Quebec City assisted by non-commissioned officers and several privates. In 1832 and 1833 Captain Henry Reid was assisted by Sgts John Brown, Daniel Cole and Warrick, and Sergeant Jenny who stayed the winter on the island. They managed the telegraph station, the commissary and sentry duty. The military commandant also signed the certificates allowing ships entry to the port of Quebec. All other personnel, both medical and civilian, served under the military commandant. At the beginning, the chief medical officer was the Inspecting Physician. In mid-season 1832, Dr. Griffin resigned this capacity in favour of Dr. François Fortier who served until the end of 1834. The Inspecting Physician boarded the ships to determine if pestilence were present. The commandant issued a permit to proceed once he had the Inspecting Physician's consent.

In later practice, the Marine Boarding Officer, not medically trained, boarded the ship and asked a series of prepared questions. Provided there were ''no more than 15 steerage passengers aboard'', he was empowered to give clearance if he was satisfied with the answers.

The Medical Officer on shore (Dr. Charles Poole in 1833 and 1834) was responsible to the commandant for the care and treatment of sick in hospital, for the passengers in the sheds, for the ordering of coffins, food, straw for beds, medical supplies from the Marine Hospital at Quebec, the burial of the dead and other duties. In 1832, Drs. Miller and Crawford assisted Poole. There was a conflict between those holding the two posts of military commandant and Medical Superintendent. A shortage of military surgeons in Quebec entailed the hiring of civilian doctors. In 1836, the commandant was ordered not to impose his opinion in medical matters; finally in 1842, the Medical Superintendent was given top authority.[7]

---

[7]   Mitchell, C.A. Events Leading up to the Establishment of Grosse Ile Quarantine Station.

At the start of the 1830s, the medical network of the Quebec region consisted of Dr. James W. Douglas, President of the Board of Health at Quebec and his several colleagues in the Quebec City hospitals, while Drs. Poole, Griffin, Miller and François Fortier worked at the Island. Before 1840, Dr. G.W. Douglas, brother of the afore-mentioned James, succeeded Poole and remained as Medical Superintendent of Grosse Ile until 1864. In Quebec, Drs. E.B. O'Callaghan, Von Iffland and Joseph Painchaud had a clinic at Près de Ville; Drs. Lyon and Leslie served at the Emigrant Hospital; Dr. Andrews and Dr. Marsden, Drs. Perrault, W.A. Hall, Joseph Skey and Joseph Morrin at Quebec City.

From 1832 until 1857, the island was a military establishment. The last successor of Captain Reid was Lt. Noble of the Royal Artillery, but the name of a Captain Scott appears also as commandant at one time. Each spring, the Military Commissariat at Quebec (under Lt. Col. Craig in 1834) asked for tenders for the various supplies, services and repairs needed at Grosse Ile. The Marine and Emigrant Hospital at Quebec was the main source of medical supplies, while individuals and companies in Quebec and in Montmagny bid for contracts to provide other necessities ranging from hay, lumber, wheels, barrels, paint and dishes, to coffins and shovels and printed forms. The soldiers were called upon to do many extraordinary duties. After a doctor on the way to inspect a ship was dumped into the water by the uncoordinated rowing of soldiers, the island commandant hired boat crews from the neighbouring islands of Ile aux Grues and Ile aux Coudres. Little by little, the island personnel took shape. The soldiers kept a flock of sheep to provide fresh meat for themselves. The stupid sheep got lost in the woods and fell off the rocks into the river. The commandant had to requisition boards from Quebec to make sheep pens.

Captain Reid wrote about conditions on the island on August 9, 1832:

Your new building is at the moment about as full as it can hold. We have upwards of one thousand emigrants on shore, between the two sheds; and there are about 1800 more at anchor, ready to take up their quarters as soon as the present occupants be got on board, which we have to effect in the course of tomorrow.

The last two days have been very favourable, and you would have been delighted to see how assiduous the poor emigrants are in availing themselves of it, in washing and scrubbing; and we hope to send them to you in a perfect state of cleanliness and purity; but I assure you it requires every body to be on the alert to preserve anything like regularity among them.

It was the military man speaking when he wrote the words "preserving regularity among them", for some of his own troops were involved in what might be regarded as excusable irregularity, as reported in the Quebec Mercury:

The military party stationed at Grosse Ile had been remarkably healthy, till an emigrant from on board one of the detained vessels, unfortunately found means to bring on shore a jar of whiskey which he concealed in the woods, where it was found by some of the detachment who drank to excess and several cases of cholera followed; one of which proved fatal. The circumstances excited much surprise; as the commandant had taken every precaution to prevent the introduction of spirituous liquors, and no clue could be obtained as to the mode by which it had been obtained till one of the patients confessed to the fact above stated and unravelled the whole affair.

1833

Immigration continued heavy in 1833. Captain Reid wrote long and leisurely reports commenting on the activities of the station from early May till the closing in October. He described the pilots setting out the buoys on May 10. He seemed to have a keen sense of the element of contagion when he forbade healthy passengers to bring meals to their sick relatives, this in contradiction to Dr. Poole's allowing it.

His reports in 1833 contain the opinion that it was "those who came on board delicate" who died. "Children died of decline and want of nourishment" he wrote. Anything but delicate was the following reported in his papers. The Brig Eliza Ann from Cork was reloading immigrants from the island. Such was the press of people to one side of the bateau that she swamped and John Sullivan from Bantry and Thaddeus Lenny from Glenville were drowned. In the investigation following the incident the Second Mate, Edward R. Good, and two cabin passengers, John and Richard Carey, gave testimony, along with Férreol Bourgette, the pilot. The sailors were disobedient, they said. The Mate was in charge of the bateau (Captain had died of cholera) and in attempting to keep order had to contend with one seaman, John Daly, who had managed to find liquor on the island, and two other equally unruly crewmen, Roger Sullivan and Edward Holmes.

In referring to the incident, Reid wrote "It is no easy task to attempt getting direct answers from these corcagian people."

In the month of October, the men of the 32nd Regiment were replaced by a detail of the 24th Regiment under the command of Captains Stack and Ewing, Lieutenants the Honourable C. Preston, Spring and Cunynghame. A sergeant and some soldiers were to stay the winter in charge of the buildings.

The military commandant's name appeared on the permits of release from quarantine, allowing ships to proceed up-river. For 1832, a large collection of those exists, evidently handed in to the Harbour Master at Quebec. The first third or so of the collection consists of printed forms with ship's name written in by hand; the remainder have been laboriously written in longhand, mute testimony indeed to a clerk's patience, but more evidence also of the great number of ships arriving and of a certain lack of preparedness for them.[8]

---

[8]   PAC — R642 II A3 Vol. 14.

There exist also reports of commissions of inquiry into the conditions of immigrants. Frequently the pilots were called upon to testify as in the previous incident of the boat swamping. Some of the pilots who brought ships into the Quarantine Ground in 1832 were: Amable Paquet, Férreol Bourgette, J.B. Turgeon, E. Antille, F. Curadeau, J. Pedick and J. Lavoie.

Despite the fact that much had been built in the midst of the busy summer of 1832, for example a Catholic Chapel and an Anglican Chapel, several hospitals and stores, — the facilities on the island were still at an inadequate minimum.

In 1833, therefore, the government provided funds for buildings to house the small garrison, the boat crew, other civilian personnel like butchers, bakers, cooks, nurses and orderlies. Requisitions flew from the island to Quebec in a storm of demands for everything from new hospitals to a new wharf, to boatsheds, to a flag staff to a sentry box!

Conditions on the island can be imagined from the list of items required in 1833. Boats were needed: "large and substantial bateaux" which could moor in the stream and safely take passengers and baggage off the ships (there was never an adequate pier for large ships); a fast boat for carrying messages to St. Vallier when the island was fogged in and the semaphore signals were invisible from Montmagny. There were requests that the rocks on the beaches be levelled to give facilities for washing and cleaning. This was not done, not even as late as 1847. Obtaining fresh water was also a problem, especially during crowded times. To solve this, there was a standing order that the steamers going between Quebec and Grosse Ile always carry the water puncheons to be filled at Quebec. Loading and unloading in midstream such an array of articles, to say nothing of passengers, both sick and healthy, presents an awesome task to the 20th century viewer, and probably daunted many a discouraged traveller in those days.

In 1832, the Catholic chapel on the island was given the name of Saint Luke. Both a priest and a minister were residents during the navigation season, for in those conventional times people took church going very seriously. The military commandant and also the Governor General's office granted the permits for the priests and ministers to travel to the island. Between 1832 and 1847, Fathers O'Dwyer, Dunn, Harkin, Huot, Belleau, Griffiths, Fréchette, Dowling, Moylan and Beaubien served at Saint Luke's. Between times, the island was a pleasant place, quite attractive even for picnic groups from Quebec. The Quebec Gazette in 1835 reported that parties of officers from the garrison with their lady friends might spend the day on the island, going and returning by steamer. The island gradually assumed its successful protective role. The exception to success was the dreadful summer of 1847 when once more the magnitude of the tragedy was beyond the powers of the station to handle.

In 1834, there was a second cholera epidemic. Grosse Ile cared for its share, but still 2900 died in Quebec City. Other cities further west were also affected that year. In that summer, five men of the 32nd Regiment died working as nurses in the hospital: William Slack, Patrick McDonagh, John Morgan, John Cahill and Thomas Greenwood. A sixth man, the telegrapher, who simply walked past the sheds daily, caught typhus (one of the many diseases present at the time) and died. Diseases like cholera again spread westward with the immigrants to the cities.

The epidemic of 1847 was typhus, or ship fever, not cholera. However, in 1849, another major epidemic of cholera swept England and was carried on the emigrant ships to Canada and reached Toronto before the end of June. Outbreaks of cholera in 1851, 1852 and 1853 were confined to the Province of Quebec. The death toll for those years did not go beyond 200 each year.

From the very beginning, the status of the island was under discussion. In 1833 the Executive Council was advised by the Attorney General, C.R. Ogden, that "it is within the competence of the Governor General to retain Grosse Ile and use it and the buildings thereon, and any of the other islands." (RG4-1833)

This was the result of an investigation into the claims before the Assembly. Notary Bernier of Château Richer claimed to be the owner and Pierre Duplain to be his tenant. According to John Jordan, in his comprehensive book on the Grosse Ile tragedy, an act was passed indemnifying them for their losses, but there is no record that they were actually paid.

RETURN of Sick treated in Hospital, from its Establishment in 1833 to September 18, 1838.

Year	Number of Passengers	Admissions					Discharges			Deaths			Remarks
		Cholera	Fever	Small-pox	Other Diseases	Total	Cholera	Other Diseases	Total	Cholera	Other Diseases	Total	
1832	51,422	No return of sick this year											
1833	22,062	—	159	34	46	239	—	212	212	—	27	27	
1834	30,982	290	404	12	138	844	132	448	580	158	106	264	...Most of the deaths these two years (which proved fatal in the proportion of 1 in 8½) were from fever.
1835	11,580	—	24	48	54	136	—	116	116	—	10	10	
1836	27,986	—	338	50	66	454	—	396	396	—	58	58	
1837	31,894	—	481	104	13	598	—	541	541	—	57	57	
1838	2,918	—	21	16	16	53	—	48	48	—	5	5	
	168,842	290	1,427	264	333	2,314	132	1,761	1,893	158	263	421	

(signed)   *John Doratt*, m.d.

Dr. George Mellis Douglas, born in Carlisle, Scotland in 1809 and died at Ile-aux-Ruaux (near Grosse Ile) in 1864. George and his brother, James, were notable figures on the medical scene in Quebec. He served at Grosse Ile from 1832 to 1864, in various capacities, but principally as the medical superintendent. The exploits of the Douglas family make interesting pages in many areas of Canada's story, from military and medical heroism to inventions to the establishment of longlasting philanthropic institutions. DCB, Vol. IX, pp. 217-18. (Picture supplied by Dr. Sylvio Leblond)

There appears to have been a Catholic Chapel on the island very early in its quarantine career. The registers of the parish of Saint Luke date from 1834. One very early entry was made on May 5, 1834, by Father J.B. McMahon: a baptism of M. Joice, son of Patrick Joice and Mary Mahoney. Later that year, on October 5, Father McMahon christened Johann Hospere, son of Johann Melecher Lyphette and Efa Lughuer (?). The latter indicates that Europeans other than from the British Isles were making their way into Canada very early. The early chapel, 30 feet by 18 feet was replaced in 1874, in an entirely new location, by a larger building 40 feet by 24 feet. (Letter from Rev. J.S. Maguire to the Bishop re a new place of worship — in Archives Dioc. St. Anne de la Pocatière.) Eventually the steeple was graced with a bell of French manufacture, in Vimy, dating from 1809.

This chapel, the Anglican Chapel, was built in 1871. The Protestant clergy were always devoted to the immigrants. There are letters from Rev. H. Sewell in both 1832 and 1837 complaining about the lack of chapel facilities for Protestants on the island.

Mary Eileen O'Gallagher Conway was the daughter of Jeremiah Gallagher. She wrote the poem ''Grosse Ile'' at the age of sixteen.

GROSSE ILE

O solitary isle — whereon a granite sentinel does stand
    For all to see, from great ships passing by,
    In memory of the thousands who did die
Upon your shore, far from their own dear native land.

O tear-drenched isle — such scenes of anguish were enacted here;
    Heart-rending moans of suffering filled the air
    And only Faith did save them from despair.
That sad, sad, sorrow-stricken year.

O windswept isle — your gnarled trees bend with the gales that sweep
    Above the hallowed ground wherein they lie
    Those exiles who sought freedom but to die;
In foreign soil they take their last long sleep.

O silent isle — could you but tell the tale
    That tragic story so few know too well
    The dire results of laws conceived in hell.
Which told today make valiant men turn pale.

O poor Grosse Ile — what awful scars you bore
    When spades dug deep into your breast
    Where speedily the dead were laid to rest
By brave Canadians who did this ghastly chore.

O sad Grosse Ile — no time for solemn funeral rites
    No incense to perfume the air
    No choir to chant a hymn or prayer
Heart-rending scenes — horrendous task, by days and weary nights.

Mourn, o lone isle — not only for the plague-wracked humans now at rest,
    History will ever link their fate with you;
    But for the clergy, doctors and layfolk too
Whose works of mercy only God did see, who now sleep still beneath your breast.

O quiet isle — where winter wraps you in a shroud of white
    And summer spreads a coverlet of green
    And turns this spot into a peaceful scene
Golden in the sun by day, silvered by moon at night.

E'en when the fog rolls in, veiling your placid face
    E'en when the wild waves toss
    Nobly there stands our Celtic Cross
Raised by the sons of Gaels — marking fore'er this holy place.

Mary Eileen O'Gallagher

45

From this aerial photo one can make out in the bottom right, the long lines of the oldest buildings on the island. These are the hospital "sheds" so-called from the earliest times. They date from 1847, and their wooden walls and roofs have thankfully withstood fairly well the ravages of time. A modern airstrip is in the back ground. To the right of the hospital sheds are several iron grave markers that date from 1903 to 1922 (see page 00). The other buildings, left, are Department of Agriculture buildings.

46

CHAPTER III

THE FAMINE MIGRATION OF 1847

The sadness of 1847 belongs to the Irish. In that year of general European famine, there were indeed many other immigrants to Canada and the United States besides the Irish — from England, Scotland, from Germany and Norway. However, the immigrant ships from Ireland and from Liverpool bore people in an entirely different set of circumstances to the new land. They carried throngs of malnourished, downtrodden, dispirited people ravaged by hunger and disease, and turbulent with political despair. The accumulation of hundreds of years of institutionalized injustice in Ireland came to an ugly culmination in 1847. This time the consequences were no longer stored in local memory in Ireland to fester there. The knowledge of horror spread tellingly into another continent and indelibly into the collective memory of generations, not only of the Irish, but of others all over North America. Nowhere is this more evident than in Quebec where the word 'Irish' usually evokes reference to the famine migrations of 1847 and the tragedy of Grosse Ile.

The failure of the potato crop in Ireland upset the delicate (and miserable) economy of an agricultural people reduced to eating one staple, potatoes, while they paid to an absentee landlord the rent from the proceeds of the only other staple, wheat. Both government and private measures to feed the people were inadequate. The people turned again to emigration as a solution. Some fled with the rent money in their pockets as soon as the wheat harvest was in. Some put their meager family savings into a ticket for one or two family members to get to America. Many were allowed and encouraged to leave by landlords eager to be rid of hundreds of tenants who were not proving profitable, and in this famine time were becoming a burden. Some tenants were 'assisted' to emigrate. The assistance sometimes was real in the form of money or sailing arrangements, sometimes it consisted of promises, not always fulfilled.

ASSISTED EMIGRATION

The calculations of the Emigration Agent at Quebec showed fewer than 7000 immigrants received assistance out of an estimated 74,000 arrivals in 1847. The percentage is small indeed, but for those 7000 and their descendants this is an unhappy memory. There is also the indication of an attitude on the part of the landlords to rid themselves of "redundant labour" or "surplus population". However, assisted emigration was not necessary. Lord Grey of the Colonial Office wrote to a relative:

> The Government cannot undertake to convey emigrants to Canada because if it were to do so, if we were even to undertake to pay part of the cost, an enormous expense would be thrown upon the treasury, and after all more harm than good would be done ... some £150 000 would have to be spent in doing that which if we do not interfere will be done for nothing.[9]

In the minds of the people, however, who were persuaded to use this means of escaping the famine, there were to remain the bitterness of the deceit, or the heartbreak of loss. A.C. Buchanan, the Emigration Agent at Quebec questioned many aspects of immigration from the British Isles. Besides questioning cabin passengers and ships' captains and crew concerning the conditions of the voyages, he also questioned why the people were leaving Ireland. One such questioning, before Robert Symes, a Justice of the Peace, took place at Grosse Ile in September 1847. The sworn depositions very quickly made their way to London and thence to Ireland, and before December of that year, denials from the agents and bailiffs in Ireland had been registered with the government in London.

DEPOSITION OF Hugh Reilley, stonecutter of Kivally, County Fermanagh

> He has wife and five children. In May the landlord Collins gave him relief. On June 1, Hugh Quin the bailiff offered him clothes for himself and his family and tickets to Quebec for all of them. They could walk to Enniskillen thence to Derry where the agent would give them the clothes. Quin bought Indian meal for the passage instead of their clothes. Captain Mason treated them with kindness and gave them biscuits. Signed at Grosse Ile 12 September 1847 R. Symes, J.P. (B.P.P. Vol. 17, p. 217)

DEPOSITION of Bryan Prior, labourer of the parish of Drumreilly, County Leitrim.

> He has a wife and four children under twelve. He farmed five acres on the estate of Collins. For six weeks before leaving he had nothing. Collins' agent Benson promised to give him relief if he gave up his land. The minute he did his house was pulled down. Then Benson said the land was of insufficient value therefore he could give them nothing.

---

[9] Quoted in Gilbert Tucker: Famine Immigration to Canada, p. 538 Lord Grey to Sir George Grey Nov. 16, 1846 Grey Emigration Papers 1823-1850.

Benson refused to send wife and children to America, it was expensive enough to send him, "and be thankful for it". The wife and children are now in Ireland without a house or a home, as far as this deponent has any knowledge of their condition and he now declares that he is in a most distressed state of mind, without money, clothing or food. Signed at Grosse Ile 12 September 1847 R. Symes, J.P. (B.P.P. Vol. 17, p. 218)[10]

QUEBEC CITY IN 1847

Both administrators and ordinary citizens of Quebec were well aware of conditions in Europe. Through 1846 and early in 1847, they followed the published accounts of the famine overseas. The advent of steam on the Atlantic had speeded up the dissemination of news as well as government dispatches. The harbour masters in the ports of Britain and Ireland made up their lists of passengers and ships' manifests and sent them by steamship to New York or other North American ports whence they were sent by railroad to Quebec. Thus it was that the Emigration Agent at Quebec knew by April 1847 that more than 28,000 Irish had left Liverpool and the Irish ports destined for Quebec. The newspaper also published another item of interest in this immigration flavoured city: the United States had doubled the cost of passage to American ports, and was confiscating overloaded immigrant vessels. While steam shipping was in its infancy, it was sailing vessels that still furrowed the ocean for many years. In 1847, every type of vessel already engaged in the timber trade out of Quebec could be offered as an immigrant ship. It was mainly these vessels, the timber ships, that carried the major part of the immigrants to Quebec.

In Quebec City there was more than the usual activity as such agencies as the Quebec Emigrant Society prepared for a larger and more needy influx. Throughout the early part of 1847, a collection was made among the parishes of Quebec and the surroundings to aid the starving of the British Isles. The Irish under the direction of Father Patrick McMahon, pastor of Saint Patrick's, had taken the lead in this collection, but were soon joined by all the citizens, English and French, Catholic and Protestant, who contributed more than £1000 in the spring to send to the poor in Scotland and Ireland. Little did they realize that soon the city itself would be actively involved with these people.

---

[10]   These statements from B.P.P. p. 217 published in London Dec '47 are followed by depositions taken in Ireland by the Hugh Quin of Ganney swearing that Reilly's statement is not true. He identifies Hugh Reilly as being from Aghernly in Fermanagh. An attempt to refute Bryan Prior's statement was sworn at Ballyconnell by Farrell Kennan, also published in London in December '47.

GROSSE ILE – 1847

The Medical Superintendent at Grosse Ile in 1847 was Dr. George Douglas who had come to that post in 1836 after a short career in Quebec City. In April, the new hospitals at Grosse Ile were ready to care for 200 sick, the average of previous years, and there was space to shelter 800 healthy people. The island still lacked a deep water pier. On May 23, Dr. Douglas reported that the hospitals already held 530 sick, and that 40 to 50 deaths a day were being recorded. The immigrants were arriving in more than usual numbers as had been foreseen only lately, and this time they were weak with hunger, and ravaged with many diseases, but particularly with typhus.

TYPHUS

This was not the first time that Quebec has suffered from typhus. Long before, in 1659, the disease had broken out on board the Saint-André from France, bound for Quebec and Montreal with 130 emigrants. Ten travelers died during the voyage and when the remainder landed, the disease spread among the inhabitants of Quebec City and a number died. At this point, all resemblance between the two outbreaks ceases. The 1847 epidemic had the quality of nightmare about it, both on the quarantine island and in the cities where the unfortunate immigrants sought refuge after their release from quarantine.

As in the story of the cholera epidemic of 1832, so in 1847 there is difficulty in ascertaining which ship brought in the first cases of typhus. Some sources say the ship Urania from Cork brought in many sick on May 8. The government lists put the ship Syria on May 20 as the first of the "fever ships" thus baldly labelled. She was 46 days out of Liverpool with 241 steerage passengers on board, 9 of whom died at sea of typhus and 40 in the quarantine hospital at Grosse Ile.

From then on the horror mounted during that extraordinarily hot summer. Additional doctors came from Quebec and from the towns along the river. Before the month of May ended, Dr. Douglas himself had fallen sick. Drs. Jacques, Fenwick and McGrath, then Drs. Clark and Landry were added to the staff. One young doctor, Benson, off the Ship Wandsworth from Dublin, volunteered to work with the doctors on the island. He died after one week.

Dr. Douglas supervised the medical work, going from one end of the island to the other both night and day, sometimes on horse back. His office recorded the numbers of ships, the numbers of immigrants brought to hospital, occupying the "healthy" tents, the deaths, the people dismissed from the hospitals. The professional men and several nurses worked loyally and steadily. For many who had come to work as assistants in the hospitals, at very low wages, the enormity and ugliness of the situation was just too much; consequently there was a constant stream of workers leaving on the steamboats for Quebec and Montreal, to be replaced by opportunists and adventurers, "profligates of the worst kind", Dr. Douglas called them, who came to prey upon the helpless.

There was, during that summer, a steady acceleration in the number of ships arriving, of immigrants (12,000 on June 1, 14,000 by June 8), of sick in the hospitals (1,100 by June 8) and an awesome list of deaths: in June, Douglas spoke of between 40 and 50 deaths a day, and this average fluctuated but little, and that always upwards.

While the hospital personnel offered what care they could in medicines and bedside attention, the clergy brought spiritual assistance to the dying and to their families. Both Catholic and Protestant clergy from Quebec City and the country parishes came to the island, worked in the hospitals and went on board the ships. Father Bernard McGauran of Notre-Dame de Québec (later pastor of St-Patrick's 1856 — 1874) was in charge of the first group of priests to go. With him went priest professors from the Séminaire de Québec, among them E.A. Taschereau, later Canada's first Cardinal. The hot summer dragged on and more priests came to the island. The clergy were very numerous, hence could rotate and allow each other some time away from the island. Bernard McGauran fell sick with typhus, recovered and came back late in the season — in fact, he was the last priest on the island when it closed for the winter. His fellow priest, Father Hugh Paisley, gave up his life working among the sick, as did many others, Catholic and Protestant, Irish and English and French Canadian. Though the number of Irish Protestants among the immigrants probably did not exceed ten percent, the proportion of Anglican clergy was considerably higher. Bishop George J. Mountain, Anglican Bishop of Montreal, twice came to the island that summer. The priests and the ministers proved to be the brave intermediaries between the immigrants and the local people, who feared the presence of the immigrant as bringing disease and death, and with good reason. The clergy found themselves obliged to care for homeless children, as children outnumbered adults 54 to one, according to some estimates. In both Montreal and Quebec there were careful records kept of them and their adoptive families.

On the island, the management of landings, the order of inspections, of housing, of food, was under the military commandant. The soldiers were supposed to police the island, keeping the healthy from visiting their relatives and friends in the hospitals. However, many other tasks fell to their lot. With the overcrowding of the hospitals, the army was called upon to supply tents and to put them up. When civilians deserted, soldiers took up their duties. One of the most heartrending of the tasks demanded of them was no doubt that of handling the dead. There being no deep water pier, all unloading of ships was done in the stream. Frequently a ship was in such a condition that no one on board could remove himself, much less lift out the dead or clean the ship. The boatmen, the soldiers and the priests therefore proceeded with the removal of bodies from the ships. One description tells of bodies, uncoffined being winched out of a hold, the golden hair of a young girl moving in the slight breeze. Once ashore a burial service was conducted and the sad record can be read today in the registers of the chapel of Saint Luke on the island.

> I, the undersigned priest, have this day buried Patrick Murphy, John Kelly, Maria Brown and forty-three others ...

Burials became an unceremonious matter after a short while. Individual graves were unknown. One great field became a common burial ground. Because of the thin layer of earth on the island, soil had to be brought over from Montmagny to fill in the trenches whose sad traces are still visible today.

The military men also supervised the loading of the immigrants on the steamers: Canada, Alliance, North America, Queen and Rowland Hill which plied the river between Grosse Ile and Quebec or Montreal. These steamers had been commissioned especially for this task. They were frequently over-crowded and typhus often broke out on board before they reached the inland cities. A whole new scenario of misery was enacted in Quebec and Montreal as the sick were sheltered in the hastily raised "sheds", usually as far away from heavily populated places as possible. The port of Montreal has its own sad story of death and devotion. Quebec, closer to the island, also shared in the sorrow of disease and death.

Dr. Douglas sent weekly reports to the Quebec Mercury. Early in June, after his own recovery from the sickness he wrote to the newspaper:

> Good God, what evil will befall the city wherever they alight. Hot weather will increase the evil ... Now give the authorities in Quebec and Montreal fair warning from me, I have not time to write or I should feel it my duty to do so. Public safety requires it.

Occasional summaries of statistics appeared:

REPORT PREPARED FOR MERCURY:

May 10 to July 24

	Men	575
Died in hospital	Women	416
	Children	467
		1,458
Died on ships from Great Britain		2,366
on ships at Grosse Ile		721
in tents near the healthy		27
	TOTAL:	4,572

This situation continued until August. Lack of shelter, lack of rest for those tending; want of ordinary comforts of home and table. The immigrants could procure food at a commissary operated by Captain Boxer of the Royal Navy who arranged the transport of food and its sale at cost, when it was realized that there was not enough food available in the kitchens of the establishment. In August, the 3,500 healthy immigrants could finally move into wooden buildings made ready for them. They awaited space on the steamers. The chapels were finally cleared and no longer had to be used as hospitals; the tents were abandoned. These were so filthy that the soldiers had to be ordered to strike them and drag them to the river to be cleaned by the current before they could be washed.

As the summer waned and the epidemic lost its size and virulence there came a report from Douglas' office to rouse indignation again in the hearts of those who had any feeling left. Douglas noted in November that the last ships coming up the river in September and October had a larger proportion of young men on board, the landlords having gotten a summer's work out of them before letting them go, or "assisting" them to emigrate.

At last the summer was over. The autumn came and gradually the station slowed down. A few sick people could not be moved from the hospitals, and remained the winter there.

WHAT COST?

The cost for this summer of sorrow came under discussion in the Assemblies of the colony and in the Parliament of London. Costs assumed by the colonies were quickly covered by the Imperial Parliament. There are some figures available in public records, but it is not the aim of this book to present such tabulations. Other costs, however, cannot be forgotten, the inestimable price of lives: lives of men, women and children thrown upon the ocean waves to satisfy the exigencies of an economic system; lives lost in the tremendous display of devotion to duty and to creed offered by the doctors and the nurses and the clergymen. Who can repay the openheartedness of the families who overcame their dread of disease to take in the orphans and shelter the homeless? On the other hand, what a burden of guilt rests upon humankind that such a tragedy happened, that it is happening today, and that it will happen again. Greed, callousness, opportunism leave a bloody path.

Fifty years later, like a people reborn, the Irish of the famine migration and their descendants were able to look at the events of Black '47. Their commemoration then was not simply a hasty gesture when they went back to Grosse Ile, but a careful recollection of the whole awesome trauma. Their preparations for a monument took nine years, but the final results, a history written and a monument unveiled before the assembled dignitaries of two nations, pointed to a new consciousness, a resurrection from the tears of the past to a strength and a solid happiness in their newfound homeland and citizenship.

REACTION TO THE IMMIGRANTS OF 1847

Usually immigration had a positive impact on the different sectors that it touched. For the owners of the timber ships it solved the problem of sending almost empty vessels westward across the Atlantic. The absentee

Irish landlords and others used emigration as a means of reducing "redundant labour" on their estates. Victuallers in the ports of departure and entry were glad to ply their trade among the hordes, for even the poorest must buy food. Many immigrants sought and found a new life, space, freedom and opportunity for work. Reports in the Upper Canada Assembly praised the arrival of the skilled craftsman and the possible investor. The Government of Lower Canada was satisfied to see the timber ships loading, especially Quebec-built ships, and gladly allotted funds to the Quebec Emigrant Society to help speed the new arrivals westward and out of the Province. In Quebec, the city fathers frequently begged for funds for compensation, for relief from the expenditure involved in caring for the flood of immigrants that doubled the small city's population almost every summer.

Quebec citizens had become accustomed to the incoming throngs, but in 1847, there is no doubt that the emigration from Ireland consisted for the most part of the poorest, the most helpless, the most victimized of people. They had been caught in a heartless system operated at a distance by pitiless men. Impoverished, brutalized, degraded, they were uprooted often on false promises, driven like cattle or lured like children away from the land whose ownership had long before been wrested from them.

Surprisingly, there was not in Canada a general uprising to refuse to accept or to assist. Instead this pathetic horde evoked a variety of reactions from the Canadian people, ranging from hostility and neglect to warmhearted acceptance and care. Humanitarians questioned the wisdom of a government that allowed landlords to "ship their redundant labour to the colonies", or what was worse to send away "the most idle, the weakest, the most unfortunate" to colonies unprepared to provide for them. Ordinary citizens banded together to offer what they could of immediate help to those lying naked on the ships. Archbishop Signai of Quebec wrote to the hierarchy of Ireland as early as June 9, 1847 concerning what his priests has already witnessed at Grosse Ile. He appealed ardently to the Bishops of Ireland to stem the tide of emigration.

In June 1847, the people of Upper Canada became aware of the sad condition of the season's immigrants. Allan McNab wrote to the Queen:

> We are most desirous to welcome to the colony all (who could be considered) proper (immigrants) but we are convinced that a continued emigration of a similar character to that which is now taking place, is calculated to produce a most injurious effect upon our prosperity. (B.P.P. Vol. 17 p. 205)

The people of the Midland and Niagara District wrote to the Queen objecting to the immigrants being "dumped" in the Canadas. They expressed sympathy for them, but in practical fashion asked for public works for their employment, and funds for orphan care. (B.P.P. Vol. 16 p. 220)

The Mayor of Montreal, John E. Mills, who himself tended the sick in the sheds at Pointe St. Charles and died in November, and City Clerk J.P. Sexton signed a petition to the Queen. Not content with simple complaints they directed blame and asked for assistance for the needy of Montreal (there were already 500 orphans in Montreal by June 23).

> That your petitioners have learned with equal surprise and pain, that some Irish landlords, among whom is said to be one of Your Majesty's ministers, have resorted to the expedient of transporting the refuse population of their estates to Canada.
>
> We cannot turn these people away famished like the Eastern United States and Liverpool did.
>
> Your petitioners most earnestly pray for relief. Montreal June 23, 1847. (B.P.P. Vol. 17 p. 204)

Despite the fact that the Colonial Secretary, Lord Grey, told Lord Elgin in 1847 to enforce "the strictest economy lest the emigrants relax in their exertions to provide for themselves", Elgin ordered that three quarters of a pound of bread and three quarters of a pound of meat be provided daily for each adult and a half pound of each per child "in the sheds" (of Montreal and Hamilton).

Besides the urgent demands for money, there were letters indignant and otherwise expressing complaints and sympathy. Many of the letter writers, spokesmen for their town or city expressed disgust that such a calamity should have been allowed to progress and grow to the proportions they witnessed. The universal cry might be said to be "Do not let it happen again". Immigration such as this could do nothing for the country. The government was being petitioned to stop the tide of emigrants.

A divine explanation offered by T. Frederick Elliot and Frederic Rogers to B. Hawes of the Colonial Land and Emigration Office, emphasizes the callous detachment of some officials in the face of the pain of people:

> We confess that after reflecting on these difficulties we are led to think that when it had pleased Providence to afflict Ireland with a famine, and consequent fever, which could not be subdued, even on the land, it was little likely that any human contrivance could have averted the same evil from the multitudes who had made arrangements for a long passage by sea. (B.P.P. Vol. 17, p. 233)

The Chief Emigration Agent for Upper Canada, A.B. Hawke, wrote from Kingston in 1847 adding his knowledge and authority to the growing wave of censure:

> Upon the whole I am obliged to consider the immigration of this year a calamity to the province. It has no doubt been the cause of much benefit to the ship and steam boat proprietors as well as to those interested in furnishing supplies for the subsistence of immigrants ... (The migrants this year) are poor, lazy, dirty, shiftless, greedy, mean with money ... Fortunately for them a great many had friends and relations settled in the province who were able to render them assistance. But for this, the calamity would have been more severely felt. (B.P.P. Vol. 17 p. 216)

Finally, from Great Britain itself came witness that the emigration from Ireland was a web of many strands. The Quebec Mercury published an article from *The Whig*, on October 26, 1847:

There is a large British force in Ireland: larger than the whole army and navy of the United States including the armies of Mexico.

At the beginning of September there were in Ireland ten regiments of cavalry; thirty battalions of infantry; two troops of horse artillery; nine companies of artillery; two companies of marines, making a total of 28,000 rank and file; plus 21,182 enrolled pensioners, militia staffs and recruiting parties. Add 11,000 constabulary and you get 60,000 men.

This British force was needed to enforce the emigration, to collect rents, to carry out evictions, to knock down houses, and to protect the convoys of wheat intended for export. Cecil Woodham Smith testifies that for the British Government in Ireland, collecting the rents cost more than the rents themselves brought in.

Only occasionally in all of the above does there appear to be any condemnation of the poor emigrants themselves. All seemed to grasp the fact that they were being victimized. More tangible, however, than absence of a certain attitude, were the actions taken by the Canadian people to care for the most vulnerable of the migration's victims: the children.

THE SAGA OF THE CHILDREN

The plight of the children, in the midst of all the horror, elicited from the adults involved the response of physical care and kindness, plus the added attention of recognition of identity. There exist lists made by church authorities both Protestant and Catholic for both Quebec and Montreal. Lord Elgin wrote: "Although the mortality among children has been very great, nearly 1000 immigrants orphans have been left during the season at Montreal, and a proportionate number at Grosse Ile, at Quebec, Kingston, Toronto and other towns." (B.P.P. Vol. 17 1847 p. 381).

For many amongst those thousands, records were kept and care given in an orphanage in Quebec City. The orphanage had been founded many years before by ladies of Quebec grouped under the title "La Société Charitable des Dames Catholiques de Québec". The ladies, both English and French speaking, ran schools and orphanages in both Upper and Lower Town. These sheltered and educated the many waifs orphaned by the hardships of each summer's immigration as well as the other orphans that were part of the population of every nineteenth century city. The establishments subsisted on the generosity of the women themselves, for the most part affluent members of Quebec society; on collections and on occasional government grants. In 1847 and 1848 someone among the ladies in the Richelieu Street orphanage recorded with meticulousness all the information possible concerning 619 orphans in their care. As will be seen in the list reproduced here (Appendix), the child's name, age, parents' names (including mother's maiden name), parish and county, and ship's name were entered, where such information was available. Another notation concerning date of entry to the orphanage, then date of departure for and return from hospital, gives

56

an idea of the routine of care that was extended to the children. For many, many entries, "died" was the last word. However, for other children, all this extremely valuable information was crowned by the column which gave the name and place of residence of the Canadians who adopted them.

This priceless document became the property of the Grey Nuns of Quebec when in 1849 they arrived, at the invitation of Bishop Pierre-Flavien Turgeon, to assume the management of the orphanage founded by the Charitable Ladies. In the hands of the nuns, it was preserved for posterity. Notations made after the name, about marriages or ordinations as late as the 1860s, show that the Sisters were interested in the careers of their former charges.

The bringing to light of this document corroborates the long standing acknowledgement that Irish orphans of 1847 were adopted by French Canadians. However, it adds an easily accepted fact: many Irish families of Quebec also adopted the children of their unfortunate countrymen.

The names, besides being entered in the orphanage register, were also recorded by Rev. F. Cazeau of Quebec who became renowned as "the priest of the Irish". In Cazeau's reports the children were listed as having been "adopted" by parish priests. The orphanage register completes the picture: evidently the parish priests, made aware of the plight of the children from both the letters and the sermons of the bishop, came to Quebec, brought the children home to their parishes where the good people took them in. Rimouski seems to dominate the list for numbers of children taken in. The reports were sent to the Bishop and to the Government in support of diocesan application for funds to care for the children. The orphanage register itself has an occasional notation: "This name was not included in the report." Documents exist of a similar nature for Montreal, for example.[11]

THE COST

The cost in humanity is beyond calculation. Thousands of lives of emigrants, mostly Irish, were lost, so were those of many of their hosts in Canada. The cost in terms of bitterness and bad memory is also very high. It almost clouds the fact that many, of many other nations came into the Saint Lawrence unscathed in 1847. It has already been noted that only ships from Irish ports and Liverpool were detained at Grosse Ile. Dr. Douglas remarked on the good condition of Scots and Germans, and of ships from some English ports.

The actual cost in pounds, shillings and pence is no easier to calculate, however some approximation is possible.

In Britain, the Emigration estimates had been doubled over previous years, from £10,364 to £23,813; this in view of the prevailing famine in

---

[11] Return (first) of Orphan Children in charge of the Montreal Protestant Orphan Asylum maintained at Expense of Government under the minute in Council 12th July 1847 PAC 4 C1 Vol. 204 File 3029-3062 in James Mangan's tender book "The Voyage of the Naparima".

Europe. In Canada the government had raised its immigration budget from £1,000 to £10,000.

Due to the absence of any easily located series of documents it is difficult to tabulate any real total accurately, but a sample is offered here of some expenses incurred:

	£	s	d
Expenses (transport, travel, maintenance) of Protestant and Roman Catholic clergy at Grosse Ile	1,270	15	0
Transport, maintenance of orphans	2,458	2	8
Salaries on Grosse Ile	21,279	5	6
Medicine and food	21,279	19	9
Burials	3,526	0	8
TOTAL	83,591	18	0

Total emigrant fund was £55,502 19 2. The remainder was supplied by the Provincial Parliament in anticipation of reimbursement by the Imperial Parliament. In addition, the buildings cost £34,950 36. This is a minimal sampling of information retrievable from the documents. (B.P.P. Vol. 17 p. 465).

Finally when another round of bookkeeping had been done and Elgin had made his reports to Britain, the Imperial Parliament, without any delay and almost in an indecent hurry voted more than £50,000 to reimburse the British North American colonies for their emigration-based deficits.

Where are the swift ships flying
    Far to the West away?
Why are the women crying
    Far to the West away?
Is our dear land infected
    That thus o'er her bays neglected
The skiff steals along dejected
    While the ships fly far away?

Thomas D'Arcy McGee

Elzéar Alexandre Cardinal Taschereau, (1820-1898) was Canada's first Cardinal. In 1847 he was a professor at the Seminaire de Québec, and accompanied Father Bernard McGauran and other priests who went to Grosse Ile. Taschereau's father had died of cholera in 1832 in Quebec, and that epidemic was always linked with the Irish – and in 1847 again, it was Irish who were most numerous if not the only ones dying at Grosse Ile.

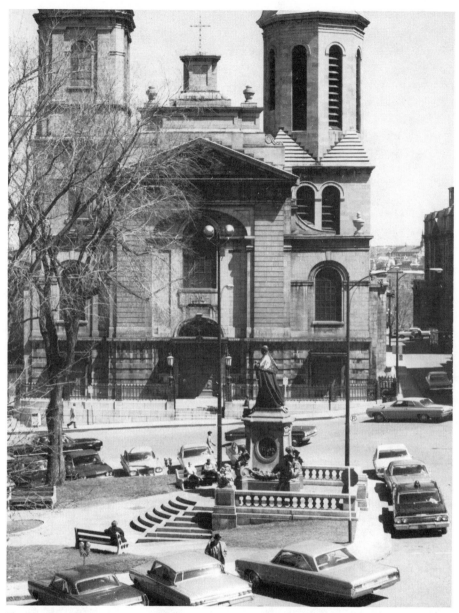

The Taschereau monument stands before the Basilica of Quebec. The Grosse Ile commemoration is on the southern face of the base. Photo W.B. Edwards Quebec.

Scene on the Taschereau monument near the City Hall in Quebec City, shows the young priest administering the last rites to a dying man. (There were no nuns at Grosse Ile) (Photo W.B. Edwards, Quebec)

Bishop Edward John Horan, born in Quebec of Irish parents. He was one of the band of priests from the Séminaire de Québec who went to Grosse Ile in 1847 to care for the sick and dying. He sickened and recovered. Later he became third Bishop of Kingston, after a career in Quebec that ranged from pastoral to university. DCB, Vol. X, 360-361.

Charles-Félix Cazeau, Vicar-General of the Diocese of Quebec, b. 1807, d. 1881. He was known affectionately as ''the priest of the Irish''. In 1847, he arranged for the shelter of many orphans, and followed their careers with interest. He was an administrator par excellence. His signature appears on reports of orphans living in the shelters in Quebec. Application was regularly made to the government for support of these children. He made arrangements for the presence of chaplains at institutions like Grosse Ile. His extensive biography in DCB, Vol. XI, p. 167-172, paints him as an administrator with a human touch.

George Jehoshaphat Mountain, b. 1789 in England, d. 1863 at Quebec. His father was the first Bishop of Quebec (Anglican) and George became the third in 1836. The tireless energy that caused him to travel, mostly on foot, from one end of his diocese to the other (Gaspé to the Red River) served him well in 1847 when he oversaw the ministry of his priests at Grosse Ile. DCB, Vol. IX, 578-581. Photo PAC 117426.

"The sheds" — the hospital buildings at the eastern end of the island. These were built in 1847, and still stand, in this 1981 photo, subject to damage from weather and creeping vegetation.

Edward Cullen Parkin: a rare photo of an Anglican priest who served at Grosse Ile in 1847. (Photo: K. & B. O'Donnell)

Alexander Carlisle Buchanan (1808-1868). Born in Ireland, he died in Quebec. He made an enormous contribution to regulating the reception and the processing of immigrants. Unfortunately, all the reports that he made in 1847, to various governments cannot be located. He worked in Quebec as Chief Immigration Agent unofficially as early as 1833, until the end of his life. DCB, Vol. IX, p. 97-8.
Photo PAC 117427

CHAPTER IV

NEW ADMINISTRATION
1857 to 1937

After the paroxysm of 1847, the island assumed its quiet but steady and vital role in the Saint Lawrence shipping picture. Immigration continued as the highlight of every summer, though the faces and the languages of the people arriving began to change. Quarantine procedures changed also and it seemed that only at times of emergency was Grosse Ile really used. As already noted, even in 1847, many ships (other than from Irish ports) were allowed to bypass the island to discharge their passengers at Quebec, or at Lévis where the railroad could take them to their inland destination. This sporadic use of the island was to result in a temporary deterioration of the facilities and services.

In 1857 there came a change in the overall administration of the island. The Imperial Government transferred the ownership and operation to the Government of Canada. The Department of Agriculture, the agency most involved in promoting immigration, assumed control. With this change, the military garrison which had carried out such a variety of responsibilities in its twenty-five year tenure was withdrawn.

Lieutenant Andrew (later Sir Andrew) Noble[12] of the Royal Artillery served as the last military commandant of the island. The medical men then became the superintendents of the island. In the beginning of the station's existence in the 1830s, Dr. Charles Poole had succeeded as medical officer after the short and strenuous terms of Doctors Griffin and Fortier. During that time, Captain Henry Reid was commandant. Poole's assistant and successor, Dr. George M. Douglas, medical superintendent during the summer of 1847, as seen in a previous chapter, saw the military staff leave the island in 1857 and himself become the first civilian superintendent. Dr. Douglas held that post until 1864.

---

[12]   Andrew Noble married Margery Campbell, a younger sister of Charlotte Campbell Douglas (Mrs. Dr. G.M. Douglas). They later lived at Newcastle-on-Tyne. At age 91, in 1925, Margery Campbell Noble wrote her memoirs under the title ''A Long Life'' privately printed at Newcastle-on-Tyne in 1925.

Dr. Douglas was succeeded in that year by his assistant, Dr. Von Iffland. Von Iffland served only five years as head of the establishment and was succeeded by Dr. Frederick Montizambert, his assistant of three years.

Including those years, Montizambert would eventually count thirty-three years' service on the island. In 1899, he left to become Director General of Public Health and Sanitary Advisor to the Dominion Government, but his connection with the Quarantine Service of Canada did not by any means end at that time.

From about 1870 on, there was a steady change and improvement in the services offered by Grosse Ile, improvement and change necessitated by the volume of immigrant traffic on the Saint Lawrence.[13] Montizambert was greatly involved in many aspects of this work: his secretaries did immeasurable paper work to keep the government, the shipping agencies and international medical associations aware of significant events and health measures. In addition, he himself trained militia men to serve in the hospitals of the island.

In 1899, when Montizambert was transferred to the Quarantine Service in Ottawa, Dr. G.E. Martineau of Quebec became superintendent. Born in Quebec City Dr. Martineau received his medical training at Laval University, and at the Pasteur Institute in Paris. He presided over some exciting times, usual for the island, until 1929, but saw the gradual slowing down in its quarantine functions. However, he had on staff as many as 43 at one time. His assistant, Dr. W.W. Aylen, succeeded him in 1929, when Dr. Martineau died suddenly.

From 1857 until the World War, immigration was still heavy. Hundreds of thousands of Europeans were attracted to Canada and the United States by the availability of land, among many other enticements. The advantages of immigration to Canada were being advertised by the combined efforts of the shipping companies and the agents of the Canadian Government in the cities of Europe. Sir John A. Macdonald needed people to make complete the triad of trains and wheat trade and travelers that he envisaged opening the West. His government and later that of Sir Wilfrid Laurier made concerted efforts to keep a steady stream of choice settlers coming to Canada.

Though immigration from the British Isles never ceased to dominate the statistics, there was by the 1880s a noticeable growth in the numbers of other national groups. The presence of Norwegians and Germans was noted by Dr. Douglas, indeed even in the midst of the 1847 horrors. In 1858, the only sickness he reported that summer was on "a Norwegian ship, with many sick aboard, crowded with baggage, agricultural implements and carrioles and barley bread, mutton, codfish and sour whey which create an impure air." (PAC RG4 C1 1858 Vol. 427 No. 238). Not all such immigrants went immediately to the interior. In more than one instance, immigrants were to get no further than the island itself: case in point, that of Andrew Andersen (sic) a Norwegian who was invited to join the police

---

[13]   Cf. Canadian Medical Association Journal, 1926, XVI 314-319 "The Story of Fifty-Four Years Quarantine Service from 1866 to 1920", by Dr. Frederick Montizambert.

force of the island in 1858 (the military had left this post as well as others). In 1859, he was promoted to interpreter, and was replaced on the police force by one Peter Wangartner, a German whose wife was Norwegian. Andrew Andersen (sic) married Julia Cannon, an Irish girl from Quebec, and was still listed on the 1881 census of the region as an interpreter. The little island was already assuming the look of a microcosmic Canada with its French backbone and its Scots, German, Norwegian and Irish residents. At a later date, a young Scottish orphan girl named Jenny would go into domestic service with the Martineau family and never leave the island.

For most of the staff of the Quarantine Island, the practice had been for the technical staff to stay only the summer — that is from the opening of the station on April 1, until the end of November. Whole families moved at these times, staying the winter at Montmagny or in Quebec City or elsewhere. In 1906, a newly arrived interpreter, the multilingual Belgian journalist, Gustave Vekeman, realizing the importance of his services, and motivated as much by his age of 65 as by a dislike of the bi-annual move, arranged with the government to stay yearlong on the island, getting light, heat and rent-free home for the winter. At that period, the summer staff could be as high as 250, while the winter residents were no more than sixty or so. A later portion of the chapter will deal with the ordinary life of the residents of the island.

CHANGES AND IMPROVEMENTS

If the island were to maintain its intended role of control of disease and epidemic and prevention of their entry into Canada, it had to evolve with the changing times, changes in both the science of medicine, as well as shipping and communications technology. Passenger comfort and safety plus national health were the ever present motives for the creativity of the Quarantine Station's administration and for their insistence on having a say in shipping practices.

In the earliest days, 1830 to 1860, Doctor Douglas had made reports and recommendations on how the laws for passenger health might be better enforced. Buchanan, the Chief Emigration Agent at Quebec, indicated how he could use Grosse Ile as an inspection site where he might confidentially question passengers, in order to ascertain whether or not the Captains were observing the various Passenger Acts. At Grosse Ile, it would be harder for them to get away, was Buchanan's opinion. It appears there was no hard and fast rule, however, concerning ships stopping at Grosse Ile. Indeed, inspection was carried on at Quebec too, and years might slip by with little activity, unless epidemics were raging in Europe. This happened often enough: Asiatic cholera in 1866, typhus in 1868, yellow fever in 1889, cholera again in 1892, bubonic plague in 1902, smallpox almost constantly, but notably in 1912. Typhus, cholera and bubonic plague as late as 1921 occurred in Central Europe, to cite but a few examples. At not one of these times did the diseases rise to epidemic proportion in Canada. The island was effectively holding its own against the entry of these virulent maladies into the country. At those times, the ships stopped at Grosse Ile and were inspected by the doctors, passengers brought ashore, the sick hospitalized, and the healthy housed until the forty day isolation period (quarantine) was over. Medical practice was gradually separating the major virulent diseases from the minor sicknesses which were sometimes called "childhood diseases". However, there were still deaths reported at Grosse Ile from such sicknesses as scarlet fever and diphtheria.

The sporadic use of the station resulted in neglect, not of medical practice, but of the physical facilities of wharf and accommodations. Improvements, repairs and additions were not being made regularly, and when an emergency occurred the inadequacies would become glaring and angry travelers would protest.

The complaints of steerage passengers might go into their memoirs or into the family reminiscences for later generations, but the complaints of the saloon passengers made their way to the Minister of Agriculture, to the Prime Minister, and to the newspapers. Passengers complained of being put off the ship, of having to carry their own baggage, of baggage lost or soaked in rainstorms; they complained of the shortage of washrooms and showers on the island. They blamed the hospitals for their illness and they blamed the doctors for the deaths of their children. On May 2, 1902, the Montreal Daily Star carried a letter from a committee speaking for the 150 saloon passengers of the Allan Line R.M.S. Ionian. Smallpox had been discovered on board and, as a consequence, the ship was quarantined at Grosse Ile and 600 steerage passengers as well as saloon passengers landed. The letter pointed out that the station was run down and dirty, and added that the complaints were being brought to the attention of the Prime Minister. Such letters, as well as the explanations and reports of the superintendents (Montizambert and Martineau) brought only stop-gap measures in the form of occasional expenditure of large amounts of money.

Meantime, while accommodations and amenities may have been neglected, there were many scientific and technical and some mundane improvements being made. In order to enable the doctors to reach the ships more conveniently, a steam yacht, the Hygiea, was at last put into service in 1886. Request for such a steamboat dated back to Douglas' time. The volume of traffic on the river was so heavy, and the yacht had proved so valuable, that within a year, another steamship, the Challenger, was added, and this allowed the doctors to board passing ships at night. The lack of docking facilities at Grosse Ile posed a perennial problem.

The ever present and always dreaded cholera spread in Europe again in 1892, and far-reaching methods were taken, successfully, to prevent its entry into this country. The bales of rags imported for paper making had long been under suspicion as carriers of disease. In 1892, under new legislation, more than 500 such bales from infected cities in Europe were burned at various ports on Canada's east coast.

No such means of getting rid of threatened infection could be used on the baggage and belongings of passengers, of course. Steam chambers were in use in Quebec and Levis at C.P.R. and G.T.R. depots, and in 1893, three new steam chambers were put into operation on Grosse Ile where they still stand, mute testimony to the work of yesteryear. Another method of disinfecting clothing and luggage was by the fumes of sulphur dioxide. There was danger of fire in this. Dr. Montizambert was able to devise a system of cooling the fumes without reducing their efficacy as a disinfectant. At about this period, the 1890s, new bathing and shower facilities were added to the station. A 50,000 gallon reservoir built on Telegraph Hill provided the necessary water for this and indeed for everyday use. A generator was installed at this time, too, and it provided for the pumping of water and for lighting of the streets. Grosse Ile was actually the first Quebec village to have electric street lights. Improvements surrounding the activity of the quarantine touched other matters: the semaphore signal system had been replaced by 1847 by underwater cable. Over the years, the annual damage to the cable by moving river ice. and the subsequent interruption of service led to the installation of a Marconi station. All these improvements brought to the island the technicians and operators needed for efficient use of the machinery.

The comfort of passengers was, in the long run, not neglected. Eventually, after many seasons of complaints, the Federal Government allotted the money for a first-class hotel and a wharf. This was done under the Borden Government when D.O. L'Espérance, the Member of Parliament (later Senator) for Montmagny called attention to the poor conditions of Grosse Ile. "In the interests of immigration and for the humane treatment of new settlers" $375,000 was spent. Two hundred men were hired for the work. By the fall of 1913, the work was done and Doctor and Mrs. Martineau played host to a visit by the Lieutenant Governor Langelier and Mrs. Langelier and their Aide-de-Camp, Victor Pelletier. Member of Parliament, D.O. L'Espérance, accompanied by his wife and daughter, guided their government visitors around the new buildings. L'Espérance also entertained the Lieutenant Governor on the steamship Montmagny. At the same time, two hundred Laval University students were given the opportunity of seeing this mysterious island. (Morning Chronicle August 19, 1913).

THE INFLUENTIAL ROLE OF THE ISLAND

In 1889, the Grosse Ile quarantine staff was able to exercise greater influence on shipping. In that year, Montizambert became medical superintendent of the whole Saint Lawrence valley. Medical inspections which might have been performed at Rimouski, or at Father Point, or at Lévis, or at Quebec, were now co-ordinated, and a better watch was thus exercised. Since minute checking of every ship was not possible, nor even necessary all the time, spot checks of some vessels, as well as regular inspections of, for example the mail boats, brought interesting facts to light. Montizambert, by such a spot check, was able to discover that many European immigrants were getting into Canada not inoculated against smallpox. In the first year of the new system, 880 persons were vaccinated aboard ship between Rimouski and Grosse Ile. (Later, on the federal scene, Montizambert, in the midst of a smallpox scare in the United States, saw to the distribution of 30,000 vials of vaccine to 300 school boards for the protection of children in Canada.)

INTEREST OF THE UNITED STATES IN GROSSE ILE

The efficiency of Grosse Ile was of interest not only to Canadians, but to the United States' government as well. In 1885, a Dr. Rouch of Chicago, a United States Officer, Quarantine Service, spent some days at Grosse Ile. He inspected the service, and approved of Montizambert's recommendations. Again in 1893, Dr. Banks and several United States marine hospital medical officers were stationed for a time at Grosse Ile inspecting buildings and methods. These tours of inspection were not a mere matter of neighbourly curiosity but were of vital importance to the immigration service of the United States, since many citizens of the American Northwest tended to blame the appearance of local epidemics on settlers arriving through Canada. Canadians themselves crossing the border were often delayed on the same grounds. These visits of American officials to Grosse Ile resulted in lessening the distrust the United States held for the Canadian inspection system. In 1894, the American Public Health Association held its twenty-second annual convention in Montreal. A number of members went down to Grosse Ile and returned to the United States convinced of the high efficiency of the Canadian quarantine system. Dr. Montizambert was well known to the Association for his work in quarantine and had been honoured with the presidency in 1891. The Association repeated such a visit to Grosse Ile in 1931 at the time of another convention; 200 members went to Grosse Ile and thence on to the Saguenay. Great Britain had four representatives in that September visit to the island: Dr. G.F. Buchanan, Sir Allan Powell, Dr. Charles Porter and Dr. James Fenton. The island staff at the time counted Dr. W.W. Aylen in charge; Dr. Pagé; Norman McL. Harris, chief of laboratory; Aimé Cousineau; Dr. Émile Nadeau, Assistant to Dr. Alphonse Lessard, Director of Provincial Hygiene Service.

Anthony von Iffland was born in Quebec City of a German father and French-Canadian mother. His practice of medicine spanned more than fifty years. Though his first love was anatomy, he worked mostly as an epidemiologist, and it was in that capacity that he succeeded Dr. Douglas, with whom he had worked, as medical superintendent. He was fearless in approaching people with any kind of contagious disease. He was seventy-seven when he died at Quebec in 1876.

Dr. George Elie Martineau was born in St. Roch, Quebec, in 1867. He was Medical Superintendent at Grosse Ile from 1899 until 1929. He studied at Laval University and at the Pasteur Institute in Paris. He married Alice Leclerc, and they brought up their family of twelve on Grosse Ile.
(Photo: Jeanne Martineau Boulet).

75

The doctors and nurses at Grosse Ile in 1909.   Public Archives of Canada

This delightful Victorian photograph shows Mme Edouard (Zoé) Masson seated with her daughters around her. Left to right, Ozeline, Desneiges, Josephine and Anna stand in devoted pose. Both Ozeline and Desneiges served as telegraph operators between 1895 and 1900. In fact Desneiges, it is fondly recounted, met her husband through the telegrapher's key.

Miss Wade, one of the nurses of
Grosse Ile.

The Quarantine   (Mme Vekeman-Masson collection)

AN INTERESTING IMPERIAL GROUP. — The above illustration was reproduce from a photograph taken at Grosse Isle, Quebec, last summer. Each person is a citizen of the British Empire, but no two were born in the same country with the exception of the two Canadians. Reading from right to left, the countries they represent are: Top Row.—New Zealand; middle row, India, Scotland, Canadien-Anglais, Channel Islands, Ireland, Australia; bottom row, Wales, Hong Kong, South Africa, Canadien-Français, England.

(Photograph by R.W. Ellis; published by permission of J.R. Aitken.,)

The Standard Montreal 1907 Vol. III, No. 5
Supplied by Eleanor Kitchen

They left us a treasure of fit and wrath
    A spur to our cold blood set,
And we'll tread that path, with a spirit that hath
    Assurance of victory yet.
                             P.W. Joyce

Men judge by the complexion of the sky
The state and inclination of the day:
So may you by my dull and heavy eye
My tongue hath but a heavier tale to say
I play the torturer by small and small
To lengthen out the worst that may be spoken.
                             Shakespeare

Honour the doctor with the honour that is his due
in return for his services; for he too has been created
by the Lord.
                             Ecclesiasticus XXXVIII

CHAPTER V

REMEMBERING

THE MONUMENTS

As might be expected, the scenes witnessed on the island evoked a desire to commemorate both the revered dead and the heroic survivors.

First among the monuments, and still standing today, is that raised by Dr. George M. Douglas to honour his medical colleagues and to pay tribute to the unfortunates they could not save.

The small marble monument, about four feet tall, overlooks the trenches of 1847 — more about it later.

A much later monument in the form of a commemorative plaque was unveiled on June 25, 1980, under the auspices of the Historic Sites and Monuments Board of Canada (Commission des Lieux et Monuments Historiques du Canada). Andrée Desilets, the board agent, along with Conrad L'Ecuyer, a Director General with Agriculture Canada, and Patrice Dionne, Quebec Regional Director of Parks Canada, officiated at the simple unveiling. The ceremony was rendered touching and additionally meaningful by the presence of Reverend Egide Sénéchal, parish priest of Ile aux Grues, within whose care Grosse Ile now lies. The most interested participant in the ceremony was no doubt Mr. Freddy Masson, who was born on the island and worked there until his retirement in 1980. Mr. Masson's grandfather came to the island as a baker in 1864 and his family and those of his children in turn were born and grew up on the island. When Freddy Masson retired, he could well speak of Grosse Ile as his island, for his custodial care surpassed mere duty to the Federal institution as evidenced by his sensitive attention to the historical aspects of the island. His instinct for conservation makes the older island installations more valuable today.

The 1980 plaque reads:

STATION DE QUARANTAINE
DE GROSSE ÎLE

En 1832, le gouvernement établit une station
de quarantaine à Grosse Île, craignant une
épidémie de choléra en provenance d'Europe.

Mais l'organisation de la station se révéla insuffisante pour enrayer le choléra et le typhus qu'apportaient les contingents d'immigrants, ce qui explique l'apparition périodique d'épidémies au cours du XIXe siècle. Conçue comme un service temporaire, sous commandement militaire, la station fut maintenue en service par le gouvernement du Canada jusqu'en 1937, alors que l'établissement fut transféré à Québec.

GROSSE ÎLE
QUARANTINE STATION

In 1832 a quarantine ground was established here on Grosse Île in an attempt to prevent the introduction of cholera from Europe. The station's medical and quarantine facilities proved inadequate in the face of the cholera and typhus which periodically accompanied immigrant ships; consequently, epidemics spread through the Canadas on a number of occasions in the mid-19th century. Originally designed as a temporary establishment under a military commandant, the station was later operated as a regular service by the Canadian government until superseded in 1937 by new facilities at Québec.

Commission des lieux et monuments
historiques du Canada
Historic Sites and Monuments Board of Canada

Most touching amid the sites of Grosse Ile are the cemeteries. The families who lived on Grosse Ile, in the parish of Saint Luke, had their family monuments in the small graveyard at the eastern end of the island. Many of the grave markers disappeared with the construction of the landing strip for the small planes that service Grosse Ile.

Close to the "sheds" of 1847, the oldest buildings on the island, is another small graveyard. The crosses still standing are of galvanized iron pipe and the name tags riveted in place are clear and stark, and can easily be read:

BURIED AT GROSSE ILE   Age

Walter H. Newton	4	S.S. Empress of Britain	1/12/1912
Anna Neuman	8	S.S. Palanza	9/12/1912
Heinrich Neuman	6	''	20/12/1912
Ella Neuman	4	''	10/12/1912
Ludwig Bromsenki	10 mos.	''	14/11/1912
Gustav Bertran	25	S.S. Scandinavian	/5/1922
Salmi Wilyo	28	Heinrich Laund	13/5/1922
J. Groves	20	S.S. Bavarian	17/7/1922

Imagda Gabrielson	2	Penrhyd	2/10/1922
Allen McCaskill	50	S.S. Montrose	23/5/1903
Johannies Ratt	1½	,,	23/5/1903
Katharina Jacob	1	,,	5/6/1903
Alexander Klein	1	,,	9/5/1903
Marie Holle	10½	,,	7/5/1903
Tim McCarthy	43	S.S. Monmouth	5/8/1903
Crinia Sapozninion	2	Lake Erie	22/8/1903

Besides these visible signs of burial, there are many other unmarked places on the island which served as graves especially in 1832 when bodies were interred in the beach of Cholera Bay at low tide, and in 1847 when those who ran amok from fever, it is said, were buried where they fell.

THE CELTIC CROSS

THE ANCIENT ORDER OF HIBERNIANS MONUMENT

That the Irish should be the ones to raise the largest monument on Grosse Ile to honour the immigrants is not surprising. Consider that the majority of immigrants in the first half of the nineteenth century were Irish. The death of thousands of their fellow countrymen in misery on that island was the sharpest memory etched in the hearts of the Irish in Canada in the late nineteenth century.

That the Irish of Quebec City at the turn of the century spurred the enterprise and carried it to a grand conclusion is not surprising either, for the events of 1832 and 1847 had made an indelible impression on the Irish of Quebec, and proximity to the island had always nudged dormant memory. Besides, the events of 1847 had forged a link between the Irish and the French Canadians.

What set the movement afoot was the fiftieth anniversary visit to the island in the summer of 1897 by a group of the Ancient Order of Hibernians. During their visit, shamed by the sad neglect of the grave-sites, they realized that they must do something. Twelve years of slow steady work ensued and finally in 1909 a monument was unveiled and a book launched, both of which served to preserve forever the memory of 1847.

ANCIENT ORDER OF HIBERNIANS

The Ancient Order of Hibernians was an organization that developed in Ireland over the centuries dating back even to the middle ages. It was more active during the times of the Penal Laws, when it became known as an association of laymen who assisted their priests in escaping from laws that endangered their lives. The badge of the order shows the hand of a priest and that of the layman in a firm clasp, the clasp of mutual help. The organization in North America was such that communication was rapid and widespread among the branches. All were grouped under one head, the National, and that comprised both American and Canadian divisions. A magazine circulated news of Irish activities both from overseas and in America among the members.

The North America AOH was first formed in New York in 1836. In 1892, a division was formed in Montreal, thanks to the work of M.J. Slattery, and in 1893, a Quebec division was founded by E.D. Redmond. The Quebec division sponsored the visit to the island in 1897, and interest in the events of 1847 began to grow.

In 1898 and 1899, letters issued from AOH Quebec Division No. 1. The secretary, Denis Coveney of Quebec City, wrote to the Department of Agriculture and on May 18, 1899 received the following reply:

> Sir:
>
> By direction of the Minister, I have the honour to acknowledge the receipt of your letter of the 10th instant, accompanied by a petition of the AOH, in Committee, praying for authority to erect a Memorial Monument on a suitable site at the Grosse Ile Quarantine Station for the purpose of honoring the graves and perpetuating the memory of their kinsmen who fell victims to ship fever in 1847 and '48.
>
> The Minister desires me to say that he has much pleasure in acceding to the wishes of the above named organization, but the charge of the ground used for the purpose of the monument would have to be subject to permission of access from the Medical Superintendent at Grosse Ile under the regular usage of passes.
>
> I have the honour etc., etc.,
> W.B. Scarth
> Deputy Minister of Agriculture

Jeremiah Gallagher, C.E., County President of AOH Division No. 1, Quebec, wrote to John T. Keating, National President in Chicago, suggesting a collection of ten cents a head from all members:

> "..... the desolate and neglected aspect of the particular portion of the island allotted for the resting place of so many of our blood and our faith seemed to strike us with reproach. After careful consideration of the matter in division meetings we have concluded that it is our duty to see that this hallowed spot where so many thousands of our country people are buried should be reclaimed, be becomingly enclosed and have a befitting monument with suitable inscriptions (in Gaelic, Latin, French and English) not only in memorium (sic) of the unhappy Irish exiles but also as a protest against the misgovernment of which they were the victims."
>
> *April 20, 1899*

Father E.A. Maguire, curé of Sillery's Saint Columban Parish, was one of the delegates to a national convention of AOH in Boston in 1900, and there he gained the approval of the group to a vote of $5000 to aid in the building. Later in Chicago, July 1908, this motion was unanimously supported and donations from AOH divisions in both countries began to come to Quebec.

THE MONUMENT

The Grosse Ile Monument Committee had a multitude of tasks to perform:

1. Raise the necessary money.
2. Design the monument, or see to its design.
3. Organize a suitable occasion for its unveiling.

The preliminary designs submitted by monument makers all used the Celtic Cross in one form or another. Based on this universal expression, final dimensions and design were made by Jeremiah Gallagher, the County President. A civil engineer, a Gaelic speaker, assistant waterworks engineer at City Hall in Quebec, he had, from the time of his arrival in Canada in 1859, become as ardent a Quebecer as he was an Irish nationalist. Reminiscences of his son, Dermot, refer to his father's scale drawing of the monument on the wall of the kitchen at 13 Conroy Street in Quebec City. As donations poured in from Canada and the U.S., the dimensions of the cross grew in splendour. A frequent visitor with the reports of donations, and with encouragement and advice was the County Chaplain, Father A.E. Maguire, of St. Columban's in Sillery. His interest was heightened by the fact that his uncle, the Reverend Edward Horan, had been one of the band of priests from the Séminaire de Québec who had gone down to Grosse Ile in 1847. Once the design and the funding had been settled, bids for the construction were called for. The international AOH magazine had published the specifications. Varying reports on the quality of granite from different quarries were received. Stanstead granite was favoured as both weather resistant and beautiful. Fallon Brothers of Cornwall, Ontario won the contract to cut the stone, transport it to Grosse Ile and build the cross there on the high ground.[14]

The work of erecting the monument was done in the spring and summer of 1909.[15] In fact, the derricks used to lift the stone were barely out of the way for the ceremony on August 15 of that year.

THE DIMENSIONS

The monument consists of a Celtic Cross of grey Stanstead granite, forty-six feet high. It stands on Telegraph Hill, the highest point on Grosse Ile, hence is 140 feet above the level of the river. The monument in the standard five sections of a classic Celtic Cross stands on a base 15 x 13 x 2 feet; above it a second base of 13 x 10 x 2 feet; the die 9 x 8.4 x 8 bears the inscriptions; the plinth is 8 x 7 x 5 feet. The shaft and cross stand 29 feet 6 inches high with an arm span of 8 feet. The topmost part of the cross is 2 feet 6 inches square.

---

[14] Fallon Brothers had the good fortune to be Irish Catholics, and to have two brothers in the priesthood!

[15] Diogene Caron of Montmagny remembers clambering over the scaffolding around the cross, as a small boy; the horse that powered the derrick was called "Boswell".

Originally the inscriptions were carved in ebony panels, but these have been replaced by granite.

The inscriptions on three sides offer the same message, in Gaelic, in English and in French:

Sacred to the memory of thousands of Irish emigrants, who, to preserve the faith, suffered hunger and exile in 1847-48, and stricken with fever, ended here their sorrowful pilgrimage.

Erected by the Ancient Order of Hibernians in America, and dedicated Feast of the Assumption, 1909.

Thousands of the children of the Gael were lost on this island while fleeing from foreign tyrannical laws and an artificial famine in the years 1847-48.

GOD BLESS THEM

This stone was erected to their memory and in honor of them by the Gaels of America.[16]

GOD SAVE IRELAND!

À la pieuse mémoire de milliers d'émigrés Irlandais qui, pour garder la foi, souffrirent la faim et l'exile et, victimes de la fièvre, finirent ici leur douloureux pélérinage, consolés et fortifiés par le prêtre Canadien.

Ceux qui sèment dans les larmes moissonneront dans la joie.

The fourth panel or memorial tablet contains the names of the devoted Roman Catholic priests who ministered to the sick and dying on the island during the terrible typhus visitation of 1847-48, those of the reverend gentlemen who were stricken down by the fever, but who recovered, being distinguished by an asterisk or star, and those among them who died from it, martyrs to their charity and zeal, by two stars, as follows:

Revd. Messrs. *William Wallace Moylan; *Bernard McGauran; James C. McDevitt; *Pierre Telesphore Sax; James Nelligan; Celestin Zephirin Rousseau; *Antoine Campeau; *Jos. Bailey; Leon Provancher; *Michel Forgues; Thomas Caron; *Narcisse Belanger; Louise Antoine Proulx; *Hugh McGuirk; *James McDonnell; *Luc Trahan; *Philippe Honore Jean; J.B. Antoine Ferland; Jean Harper; Bernard O'Reilly; Louis Adolphe Dupuis; J. Bte. Perras; Moise Duguay; Maxime Tardif; Michael Kerrigan; John Caulfield O'Grady; *Elzear Alexandre Taschereau; *Edward John Horan; Pierre Beaumont; Etienne Payment; Etienne Halle; Jos. Hercule Dorion; *Charles Tardif; Antoine Lebel; Prisque Gariepy; William Dunn; Godfroy Tremblay; Ls. Stanislas Malo; **Hubert Robson; **Pierre Roy; **Hugh Paisley; **Michael Power; **Felix Severin Bardy; **Edouard Montminy.

---

[16] In 1957 repairs were made to the cross under the direction of Dermot I. O'Gallagher, Q.L.S., of Quebec, son of Jeremiah, the designer. The AOH in both Canada and the U.S. supplied the funds.

Father Hugh Paisley, who was of Scottish descent, was not among the priests at Grosse Ile, but caught the disease while attending fever patients in Quebec and died there.

The ceremony of August 15, 1909 was as solemn in its grandeur and dignity as the event it commemorated had been grim and miserable. The Apostolic Delegate, Antonio Sbaretti, performed the actual unveiling before a throng of close to 9 000. Archbishop (later Cardinal) Louis-Nazaire Bégin preached, as did the Apostolic Delegate, and Father A.E. Maguire, AOH Chaplain. Father John Hanley CSSR, pastor of St. Patrick's, Quebec, celebrant of the requiem mass, also preached.

The occasion called for reflection, and many were the reflective comments made that day. Besides the clergy, many statesmen were called upon to speak. Sir Charles Fitzpatrick, Chief Justice of Canada, Quebec born, and Charles Murphy, Secretary of State for Canada, addressed the patient throng. Present among the dignitaries were: Hon. C.R. Devlin, Hon. John C. Kaine, M.J. Walsh, M.P.P., Wm. Power, ex M.P., E.B. Devlin and Quebec aldermen Joseph A. Collier, Patrick Hogan, W.J. Mulroney, Rev. Derome, curé of Grosse Ile, the President of the AOH, Jeremiah Gallagher, his wife Marianne (Corrigan), his two children, Dermot and Mary.[17] The American Irish were well represented. Major A.T. MacCrystal (formerly of New York 69th Reg't) couched his thoughts in Gaelic. Matthew Cummings, National President AOH, spoke as well.

The people themselves came from Quebec City and its environs of course, but also from Montreal, Ottawa, Toronto, Winnipeg, Edmonton, Calgary, Vancouver. The U.S. sent AOH delegates from Maine, Massachusetts, New Hampshire, Vermont, New York, Rhode Island, Connecticut, Wisconsin, Pennsylvania, Michigan, Illinois and Colorado.

At Quebec, between eight and nine thousand people had boarded seven steamboats Alice, Druid, Murray Bay, Polaris, Queen, Arranmore and St. Croix, for the cruise down the river to the little island. The day was sunny and warm, and as it progressed, grew steadily warmer. The photographs of the time show umbrellas raised to ward off the sun and faces being mopped free of sweat.

Men, women and children, some descendants of the survivors, French and English speaking, American and Canadian, priests and lay people, united to ponder the meaning of the past — the death and the misery — and the event in which they were sharing — the expression of sorrow and gratitude. The Requiem Mass was celebrated in the field of the graves, a rough field where the trace of trenches can still be found.

The speakers touched the well known aspects of the history of Ireland and of the Irish of Canada and the U.S., but naturally their thoughts and words converged on 1847 and its events.

---

[17] The interpreter Vekeman, as an island employee, took his seat on the dignitaries' platform and kept with him his little daughter, Jeannette, who would later write "Grand' Maman raconte la Grosse Ile".

In the presence of some few actual witnesses of those days (sixty-two years before) and of many of their descendants, the twofold role of the clergy was eulogized. The sermons and the inscriptions honoured first the sacramental presence that the priests offered at the risk of their lives to the sick and the dying. Their names are there. The crowd tacitly testified to the second role of the diocesan clergy, that of rescuer of the orphaned children, for there were among the participants, that day, several French speaking people who could say: "Yes, I was taken as a nameless child from this island and given to a family who did not let me forget that I was Irish."

In addition to gratitude to French Canadian clergy, the principal theme expressed in the inscriptions and elaborated in the speeches and sermons was that of the terrible sufferings of those people, and the desire of their descendants to honour them with an everlasting memorial.

For many a summer after that event the Ancient Order of Hibernians sponsored an annual pilgrimage from Quebec City to the Monument. There is no doubt that more than one generation realized the significance of the events commemorated and had their memories formed by the solemnity of the ceremonies carried out there each year.

There are, of course, other monuments on the island, less imposing perhaps, but nonetheless significant reminders of times, events, and the people who endured them.

The aforementioned stone pillar raised by Dr. Douglas overlooks the trenches of 1847. As far as Dr. Douglas knew, there were some five thousand people buried there. Later calculations add to that number. Nonetheless, the marker pays tribute to the heroicity of medical men — veterans on the scene and the volunteer newly arrived on the fever ships themselves.

> To the memory of Alfred Panet, medical officer of this establishment, who died of cholera, July, 1834. Dr. Robert Christie, medical assistant, who died of typhus in this hospital on the 2nd July, 1837.
>
> In this secluded spot, lie the mortal remains of 5,424 persons who, flying from pestilence and famine in Ireland, in the year 1847, found, in America, but a grave.
>
> To the memory of Dr. Benson of Dublin, who died in this hospital on the 27th May, 1847.
> Dr. Alexandre Pinet, of Varennes, died on 24th July, 1846.
> Dr. Alfred Mailhot of Verchères, died on 22nd July, 1847.
> Dr. John Jameson of Montreal, died on the 2nd August, 1847, aged 34 years.
> These gentlemen were assistant medical officers of this hospital and all died of typhus fever contracted in the faithful discharge of their duty upon the sick.
>
> Erected by Dr. Geo. M. Douglas, medical superintendent, and eighteen medical officers on duty in 1847.

More modest yet than Dr. Douglas' memorial to his colleagues, and less easily found, is a plaque placed in the Anglican Chapel. On the south wall of the sanctuary, it reads:

In Memoriam

In memoriam of the thousands of people
of many races and creeds, who, victims of
pestilence, lie buried in nameless graves
on this island.

The presence of the Anglican Church on the island dates from the first decade of the quarantine station. Anglican clergymen served the church every summer during the immigration season. In 1847 Anglican ministers laboured gallantly among the sick and the dying on the island. They had come from the city and from many of the country parishes within a very wide radius of Quebec City. Of the fifteen listed here, two died: Richard Anderson and Charles J. Morris. Others were Edward Cullen Parkin, John Butler, Charles Forest, John Torrance, Richard Lonsdell, William King, Charles Peter Reid, George Mackie, Charles Rollit, Edward G. Sutton, Andrew T. Whitten, Narcisse Guerout and Charles Morice.

These men had been encouraged and indeed abetted in their good deeds by their Bishop, George J. Mountain, who during that fateful summer of 1847 had travelled back and forth between Quebec and Montreal and the island in untiringly kind attention to those calling for his care.

There are many touching sights on Grosse Ile, but the plain and desolate cemeteries are the most subtly disturbing. The largest is simply a burial field commemorated more by the awful actuality of undulating mounds than by any crosses or tombstones.

These are deliberate or at least visible signs and commemorations of the people and the events of the century of Grosse Ile's existence as a quarantine station.

Amidst all these signs of remembrance one is struck by the contrast between the busy nineteenth century days and the present time when the quiet of unspoiled nature enfolds the few visitors.

Besides the named and the nameless remembered for their tragedy, there are also the hundreds of unsung heroes and heroines, those who, in their everyday tasks of providing the essential services, made possible the continued existence of Grosse Ile as a place of successful quarantine. These workers overcame dread of disease and fear of death to perform jobs that were at times grand and challenging and at other times humdrum and, no doubt, boring. No monument stands to honour them. Yet a monument was merited and an accolade was earned. May this book bring to mind those unsung heroes, and in its own way, draw attention to them and thus serve as their monument. They, the nurses, cooks, ambulance drivers, sentries, policemen, carpenters, painters, chore boys, grave diggers, farmers, boatmen, orderlies, messengers, telegraphers, interpreters, clerks, lab assistants, bakers, teachers and others, contributed to the existence and hence to the history of Grosse Ile.

The small monument raised by Dr. Douglas and his colleagues. It is on a little hill overlooking the field which served as the largest burying ground in 1847. Cholera Bay is in the far background.

The Celtic Cross on Telegraph Hill before the unveiling on August 15, 1909. The heat of the day is evident in the shirt sleeves and the umbrellas. A forerunner of the Quebec flag flies at the right. The flag at the left is the green banner with the harp of Ireland.

A GREAT CANADIAN MEMORIAL GATHERING—"Silently the worshippers listen; and watch the flashing of the sun on the rich vestments of the clergy." An American flag and the red ensign, (then the flag of Canada) are visible to the left in the photo.

The Standard (Montreal) August 28, 1909

August 15, 1909 The devout pilgrims at Mass, kneeling in the cemetery. The day was extremely hot, and the least shade was appreciated. Out of deference to the sacred ceremony many men are bare-headed, while others shelter their heads from the sun with the hat tilted so that their heads are not covered entirely. PAC 66298 from the Montreal Standard of August 28, 1909. The plumed helmets are those of the Hibernian Knights from New Brunswick and Ontario. Their drawn swords indicate the most solemn part of the Mass, the Consecration – hence they salute.

This plaintive picture is another in the coverage offered by the Montreal *Standard* on August 28, 1909. It is simply titled: "Old men gaze at the Celtic Cross." PAC 65177

A GREAT CANADIAN MEMORIAL GATHERING—A panoramic view of the great concourse on Grosse Isle of Perth, and National Director of the A.O.H., addressing the audience on Telegraph Hill.

Ever Befell a People Sailing to Canadian Shores

at the unveiling of the monument in memory of the thousands of victims to the ship fever. Mr. C.J. Foy, Mayor

The Standard Montreal Vol. V, No. 35, Aug. 28, 1909.

Jeremiah Gallagher, C.E., born in Macroom, Ireland in 1838, came to Canada about the age of 21. He was an active member of the Ancient Order of Hibernians and designed the final version of the Celtic Cross. He became President of the Quebec Branch of the AOH in 1908.

Father A.E. Maguire, Pastor of St. Columban of Sillery, was Chaplain of the AOH during the time of the building of the monument. His uncle, Bishop E.J. Horan had been at Grosse Ile in 1847, and Father Maguire was to serve as Chaplain there in 1871. Maguire Avenue in Sillery is named for him.

Excursion to Grosse Isle.

These photos, supplied by Jean Egan Gagnon, show a pilgrimage of the AOH in 1925. By that time, the pier could receive large steam yachts. Substantial brick buildings stand on the pier.

100

In 1925, the Hibernian Cadets' Brass Band accompanied the pilgrims. On more than one occasion an event like this had to be postponed when the quarantine authorities received word that ships were arriving with sick on board. The large buildings in the picture testify to the importance of the Grosse Ile operation.

Jean Egan Gagnon Collection — 1924 Pilgrimage of AOH to G.I..
The people formed a procession on the pier and marched to the vast cemetery where Mass was celebrated. The Hibernian Cadets leading, carry a huge floral offering. They are succeeded by the acolytes and the clergy, and the throng of the faithful.

The priests were vested in black for the Requiem Mass.

Stirring speeches as well as ho-melies were delivered after the wreath was placed on the mo-nument. Here Martin Egan ad-dresses the pilgrims. Father Meehan waits.

Matthew Cummings, National President of the AOH in 1909, returned for the pilgrimage in 1925.
Photo: Jean Egan Gagnon collection

SACRED TO THE MEMORY OF
THOUSANDS OF IRISH EMIGRANTS
WHO, TO PRESERVE THE FAITH,
SUFFERED HUNGER AND EXILE,
IN 1847-48, AND STRICKEN WITH
FEVER ENDED HERE THEIR
SORROWFUL PILGRIMAGE.

ERECTED BY THE
ANCIENT ORDER OF HIBERNIANS
IN AMERICA
AND DEDICATED
FEAST OF THE ASSUMPTION
1909

This is the southern face of the monument. Originally intended to be carved in ebony, the four panels are in dark granite. The young lady is the great grand-daughter of Jeremiah, the designer of the monument. Kathleen's picture was taken on August 15, 1982.

Repairs to the monument were undertaken in 1960. Pictured above are Dr. Larkin Kerwin and Dermot I. O'Gallagher, Q.L.S. Eddy Boulet was the Contractor from Montmagny who performed the repairs, replacing a large piece of the halo that had been damaged during a bad winter storm. The Ancient Order of Hibernians of Canada and the United States supported the efforts made to keep the monument in good condition.

CHAPTER VI

A NEW VOCATION

Grosse Ile seems to have exercised its last real utility as a quarantine station for immigrants during the time of the first World War. A few statistics illustrate the volume of traffic on the river: in 1901, four hundred vessels stopped at Grosse Ile for examination; in 1914, two hundred and ninety-one with a total of 108 613 passengers aboard; in 1916, there were even more: three hundred and forty-three with 27 973 people aboard; and in 1917, 30 127 immigrants aboard three hundred and forty-nine vessels.

In the nineteen twenties however, there was a sharp decline in the use of the island. Two or three factors could account for that: "Radio pratique", the use of radio by ship captains, and by river pilots, was made whenever there was a problem involving health which could not be solved by the ship's doctor. By radio, from the Gulf of Saint Lawrence, the captain could arrange for a doctor to come on board at Father Point with the pilot. Ships bypassed Grosse Ile and stopped at Quebec whence the sick were transported back to Grosse Ile by steam launch. Another factor in diminishing Grosse Ile's role was the desire of the steamship companies to bring their passengers all the way up the river to Montreal. They did not want to stop even at Quebec, much less at the dockless Grosse Ile. Contracts between the government and the shipping companies were being renegotiated. Many companies preferred Montreal. Even so, Quebec City was refurbishing its immigrant reception facilities with a new hospital at Savard Park.

As the medical work on the island decreased, some staff members began to look at the history of the island. There are several letters in both the Public Archives and in Church Archives, concerning the disinterment of bodies from the cemetery in 1922-1930, in order to relocate and better identify them. This applied only to the small cemeteries at the east end of the island, for the large field of trenches dating from 1847 with its thousands of Irish could never be adequately marked.

AN ISLAND VILLAGE

Jeannette Vekeman Masson, in her delightful book "Grand'Maman Raconte la Grosse Ile" paints a picture of very ordinary life on the extraordinary island. Combined with the reminiscences of others who lived or worked on the island, a picture emerges of a Canadian Village with all which that entails and more: a Catholic and a Protestant church, each with its accompanying presbytery or manse, the Marconi station, the doctors' houses with their gardens both ornate and practical, the school house, the rows of houses along a stony street, the piers where children were not to play and the beaches and rocks where they did. The children roamed the island freely, except for the occasional times when passengers from ocean liners were quarantined. Then the residential quarter became their own quarantine. Lucienne Masson remembers when the sick would go to the hospital and the healthy stayed at the hotel. She remembers forty boats in the river at a time. "Papa worked night and day", she said of her father who drove the ambulance. There were steamboats twice a week for Quebec to take the passengers to the railway depots for their trip to the interior. It was impossible to stop the children from meeting new people however; giving a rose from the garden was a good way to start a conversation. The happiness of passengers released from quarantine was thrilling to watch.

People from many nations stopped at the island and Lucienne remembers them putting on colourful shows and concerts, but no theatricals could substitute for the unrestrained joy of pilgrims ending quarantine. This contrasted sharply with the old stories the children knew about earlier times on the island. They shivered at the memory of people being buried where they fell, of loads of earth being brought across the water from Montmagny because the island's soil was too shallow for decent burial, of rats overrunning the graveyard. (Even in the 1900s, hunting rats was one of the children's adventures.) In addition to interesting passengers there were the interpreters, Mr. Beauregard, and Mr. Vekeman and Mr. E.A. Bogaert who spoke French, English, German and Italian, (Mr. Bogaert's wife was a nurse), Mr. Riopelle, the Protestant minister, Miss Rousseau, the school teacher, Sara Wade, Misses Smith and Cullen, the English nurses, and Mrs. Lindsay, the American nurse. Mr. Chevron was the telegraph operator. Antoine Létourneau was the carpenter at Grosse Ile until 1911 when a change of government affected government employees all the way down the line from Ottawa to the carpenter in way-off Grosse Ile.

Interviews with people who grew up on the island reveal a peaceful life style — normal family life carried on with the acceptance of the island's conditions as totally within the ordinary scheme of things. Mrs. L.N. Boulet (Jeanne Martineau), whose father Dr. Martineau was medical superintendent from 1899 to 1929, remembers that a young Scottish orphan girl named Jenny (Jane Robson was her name) was adopted by her family and spent her lifetime as part of the domestic staff of the Martineau family.

One family with a three generation interest in the island is that of Freddy Masson. Mr. Masson's grandfather, Edouard, was baker on the island in 1864. In 1897, Edouard's son Pierre (Pit) became the ambulance driver. Freddy and his sister, Lucienne, still recount the time their father took twenty people off a ship to bring them to the hospital. When they arrived at the hospital, there were twenty-one riders, for a baby was born in the short drive from the pier to the hospital.

The families growing up on the island were served by an elementary school. There was a school on the island as early as 1849. In 1870, the people on the island asked for a bilingual teacher. Children were shipped off to boarding school when age and season dictated it, but youth and summertime meant that the children roamed the forests and the beaches or went fishing in the Saint Lawrence with an occasional jaunt across the water to Montmagny.

Grosse Ile in the twentieth century still had its share of tragedies, as can be seen by an account of a coroner's inquest into the death of four boys: James Holland, William Mahon, John Brier, all thirteen years old, and their twelve year old companion, William Ulis. The coroner, Joseph Cloutier, M.D. of the District of Montmagny, questioned three workers from the island to try to gather the facts. Auguste Gamache, Pierre Masson and Joseph Hamel said they had told the boys not to go out in the boat, that the current was too strong for them. The boys did not heed the warning, drowning as a result. In summing up his investigation and in reply to the Catholic Emigration Association of Birmingham, England, which had custody of the boys on their way to St. George's Home in Ottawa, Dr. Cloutier said that the deaths were accidental, the boys being old enough to know better, especially after having been warned. Far from allowing any shadow of blame to be attached to the quarantine staff, Dr. Cloutier added: "Grosse Ile is not a jail."

Other visitors, besides immigrants, made island life interesting. A highlight of the period between the World Wars was the annual Irish pilgrimage from Quebec City. Organized by the Ancient Order of Hibernians almost every year, it assembled men, women and children for a prayerful boat ride down the river, a somber visit to the monument on Telegraph Hill and a Requiem Mass in the huge cemetery. This, and a summer pilgrimage to Sainte-Anne-de-Beaupré prevented any dull routine from settling into the life of this village. Besides, there were frequent individual or family jaunts by small sailboat across to Montmagny for mail or supplies. There could be little psychological isolation on this island where physical isolation was sometimes the rule of the day.

THE CLOSING OF THE STATION

Little by little the quarantine work of the island was phased out. By Order-in-Council PC 2119, August 13, 1937, jurisdiction over Grosse Ile was transferred from the Department of Pensions and National Health to the Department of Public Works. Various pieces of equipment were destined for other stations of the quarantine service, but a slight postponement was made when Quebec City Immigration Hospital was not ready and there were still people under observation on the island in that summer of 1937. The year 1938 saw the final dismantling of the station. The file closed in January of 1939.

One hundred and five years of unique service thus came to an end. The island had received hundreds of thousands of immigrants in those years. At two tragic times, thousands of those pilgrims sadly found a final resting place there. At other times, individuals were bereft of a loved one and endured a sad separation on their way into the new land. The global picture, however, if such is possible, is one of mainly successful effort. The quarantine station, originally planned as the outer defence of a country against one specific disease served over a long career to temper the ravages of many diseases, and to prevent with increasing success the entry of others into the nation that depended so much upon immigration for its expansion.

In the fall of 1937, the Quebec City newspapers noted the closing of Grosse Ile: ''With the closing of this season's navigation, the Quarantine Station at Grosse Ile has been in its 105th year of service, having been opened in 1832. The Quarantine has been officially closed these last days when the thirteen servicemen who were there left. As for the equipment which was left over, it has been transported either to Halifax or to Ste. Anne de Bellevue. In the course of these last years this station had been in the charge of Drs. C.H. Laurin and Ch. Chrétien.''

Thus ended one hundred and five years of the history of one station in one sector of Canada's Quarantine Service. Grosse Ile's years from 1939 to today are outside the scope of this book. They do warrant attention, however, for though its vocation changed, Grosse Ile's value did not. The laboratories of the island continued in use for the protection of the health of Canadians. It served as an animal quarantine station for many years and as a teaching facility for veterinarians.

Now perhaps its role will change again. Perhaps its visible charm and invisible pathos will be revealed to an interested public. Perhaps its new role is to remind Canadians of their immigrant roots and how much the tree sprung from those roots has grown and flourished.

A WORD ON THE SOURCES

Like any other producers, authors stand on the shoulders of the pioneers who went before them. There is no doubt that John Jordan's book is a well of information concerning one year in the history of Grosse Ile. "The Grosse Isle Tragedy and the Monument to the Irish Victims 1847" was issued at the time of the unveiling of the monument in 1909. It was influential in informing Quebecers about the events of 1847, and also in forming the mind-set of many people concerning the origins of the tragedy. I have used Jordan. However, I have tried to place the events of Jordan's book within the longer and larger story of the island's one hundred and five years of quarantine service.

The National Archives in Ottawa have all the necessary pointers and indicators to richer sources than I was able to touch. However, the accessible material is very rewarding: the RG4C1 files and Department of Agriculture sources have matter for deeper study.

Diocesan sources yield information on two groups of people: the children who passed through the island, and the clergymen who looked after them.

In the Appendices are gathered copies of fascinating material that speaks for itself.

The newspapers of Quebec city, as might be expected in a city so strongly influenced by shipping and immigration every summer, are a very good source of the day by day events, with frequent mention of the Quarantine Station.

BIBLIOGRAPHY

MANUSCRIPT SOURCES

Record Group 4, C1 in National Archives Ottawa.

Correspondence of AOH c 1909, in author's possession.

"Liste alphabetique des orphelins dans l'Asile Catholique de Québec 1847"
    in Archives of the Sœurs Grises, Beauport, Quebec.

PRINTED SOURCES

British Parliamentary Papers; Irish University Press, Dublin.

Dictionary of Canadian Biography, Vol. IX, X, XI.

Lloyd's Register of British and Foreign Shipping from July 1, 1847 to the
    30th June 1848: London, J. & H. Cox, Brothers, 1848.

PRINTED WORKS

Béchard, A., Histoire de la Grosse Île: Montmagny, 1879.

Cowan, H.I., British Emigration to British North America; the first hundred
    years, Toronto: University of Toronto, 1961.

Drapeau, Stan, Histoire des Institutions de Charité, Bienfaisance et d'Education
    du Canada 1878.

Drolet, Antonio, La ville de Québec, Histoire Municipale II, Régime Anglais
    jusqu'à l'incorporation 1759-1833: Québec: La Société Historique de
    Québec, 1965.

Godfrey, Charles M., The Cholera Epidemics Upper Canada, 1832-1866,
    Seccombe House, Toronto 1968.

Jordan, John, The Grosse-Ile Tragedy and the Monument to the Irish Fever Victims 1847. Quebec: The Telegraph Printing Company, 1909.

Kennedy, Robert E. Jr., The Irish — Emigration, Marriage, Fertility: University of California Press, 1973 Berkeley.

Lacelle, Claudette, The British Garrison in Quebec City as described in newspapers from 1764 to 1940; National Historic Parks and Sites Branch Parks Canada, 1979.

Leblond, Sylvio, Né à la Grosse-Ile, Cahier des Dix, Québec, 1975.

Lemoine, A.M., Quebec Past and Present 1608-1876, Quebec, Augustin Côté et Cie 1876.

------------, Picturesque Quebec, A Sequel to Quebec Past and Present; Montreal, Dawson Brothers Publishers, 1882.

Marsden, W., M.D., Plan of Quarantine for Cholera, Quebec, 1866.

Masson, Jeannette Vekeman, Grand-Maman raconte la Grosse-Île; les Éditions Laliberté, 1981.

Notman, W., Portraits of British Americans with biographical sketches by Fennings Taylor, Montreal: William Notman, John Lovell Printer, 1868 Vol. III.

Potvin, Damase, Le St. Laurent et ses Îles, Histoire, Légendes, Anecdotes, Description, Topographie, Québec 1945, Les Éditions Garneau.

Les Soeurs de la Charité de Québec, Une fondatrice et son œuvre, Maison Mère des Sœurs de la Charité, Québec, 1939.

Woodham-Smith, Cecil, The Great Hunger, Ireland 1845 to 1849 Harper & Row New York 1962.

NEWSPAPERS

The Quebec Gazette
The Quebec Mercury
The Quebec Morning Chronicle
Le Soleil
Le clergé Canadien-Français Revue Mensuelle

BIOGRAPHICAL MATERIAL

The names listed in the next page or two are presented for interest's sake. These are the people to whom the book is dedicated. They and their unnamed companions made the history of Grosse Ile happen.

PILOTS

These names appear on passes issued in 1833: Ferreol Bourgette and Amable Paquet; in 1837: Jean-Baptiste Turgeon, E. Antille, J. Pedick, F. Curadeau and J. Lavoie.

INTERPRETERS

Andrew Andersen	Peter Wangartner	Gustav Vekeman
E. Bogaert	William Alexander Brautigan	

NURSES

In 1847 Mrs Garneau and "several nurses died after they left the island". A few names of later nurses come down to us: Beaudry, Wade, Smith, Cullen and Lindsay.

DOCTORS

1832-38	Charles Poole	Harkness
	Miller	François Fortier
1841-	Joseph Parant	

1836-1864	George Mellis Douglas
1866	Joseph-Alfred Lachaine
1864-1869	Anthony von Iffland
1869-1899	Frederick Montizambert
1899-1929	G.E. Martineau

In 1847 many doctors served on the island: Jacques, Fenwick, Allen, Laroque, Malhiot, Pinet, Dease, Dickinson, Damour, Jamieson, Robert Christie, Johnston, Landry, John Racey, McGrath, Benson, Reid, a student; Barter, an apothecary. In the 20th century: W.W. Aylen; Heagerthy, J.B. Piegay Côté.

MILITARY

From 1832 until 1857 the military were involved with command of the island and with many and varied duties. A few names were found:

1832:	Commandant Henry Reid.
	Sgt Warrick, Sgt Cole, Sgt Bowden, Sgt John Brown of the 20th Regiment
	Sgt Jenny of the 32th Regt spent the winter on Grosse Ile.
	Private William Gerry was a nurse.
1834:	There was a second cholera epidemic and the following soldiers died caring for the sick: William Slack, Patrick McDonagh, John Morgan, Thomas Greenwood and William Rose (telegrapher).
1839:	Major Swinburne.
1847-1849:	Captain F.G. Scott.
	Captain Reeve.
1847:	Fifty men of the 93rd Regiment under Lieutenant Stoddard e.g. Sgt. John Rapson & William Addy of 2nd Battery Grenadier Guards, Captain Edward Boxer R.N. was Commissariat officer.

Lieutenant Andrew Noble of Royal Artillery was the last military officer in Command on Grosse Ile in 1857 when Department of Agriculture took over.

APPENDIX I

LIST OF ORPHANS

APPENDICE I

LISTE DES ORPHELINS/ORPHELINES

b. = born, né
m. = married   Died = décédé
First part: children of the 1847 migration who came into the orphanage
    between summr 1847 and early spring 1848.
Second part: children of the 1848 immigration.
Première partie: les enfants qui sont rentrés entre l'été 1847 et le printemps
    1848.
Deuxième partie: enfants de l'immigration de 1848.

ALPHABETICAL LIST OF ORPHANS
IN THE
CATHOLIC ORPHANAGE OF QUEBEC
1847

The following pages are taken from a register kept in 1847 and 1848. The book is a treasure of names of children and other information concerning them. The book is a large register, measuring about 24 by 36 inches, linen pages, heavy card covers. It was kept by "La Société charitable des Dames catholiques de Québec" when they operated an orphanage and school in Quebec City. They had been carrying on their benevolent work for several years, when Bishop Pierre-Flavien Turgeon felt the need to replace them with the Grey Nuns of Montreal. Mother Marcelle Mallet arrived in 1849 with three Sisters who took over the orphanage and school. Fortunately for historians and genealogists today, the previous institute's records were kept, and this list is now brought to light, with heartfelt thanks to the Grey Nuns, Les Sœurs de la Charité de Québec. There are 619 names, along with those of the people who adopted them.

ÉTÉ 1847 / SUMMER OF 1847

No. Rég. Reg. No.	Nom Name	Âge Age	Date d'entrée Date of Entry	Père Father	Mère Mother	Paroisse Parish	Comté County	Bateau Vessel	Adopté par Adopted by
443	BARBER, Mary Ann	1	03/13/48	?	?	?	?	?	Ant. Decaneaux Faubourg St. Roch
27	BIBLE, Ellen	10	07/47	?	?	?	?	?	Décédé/Died Aug. 6
26	BIBLE, Michael	12	07/47	?	?	?	?	?	Décédé/Died Aug. 9
73	BIBLE, Mary	17	08/03/47	?	?	?	?	?	Décédé/Died
28	BIBLE, Richard	6	07/47	?	?	?	?	?	Décédé/Died July 28
381	BOYLE, Mary	15	10/09/47	Daniel	Mary Harkin	Sligo City	Sligo	Chs Richard	Décédé/Died Oct. 29
342	BOYLE, Mary	14	10/04/47	Philippe	Mary Martin	?	Armagh	St. John	Décédé/died
62	BRADLEY, Judith	9	07/47	?	?	?	?	?	James Roach Canardière
102	BRADLEY, Judith	9	08/11/47	?	?	?	?	?	William Davis Champlain Street
356	BRADY, Francis	10	10/06/47	Andy	Margt. McGauran	?	Fermanagh	Superior	Left Oct. 26 for Broklyn
139	BRENNAN, Anne	13	08/18/47	Thomas	Briget Queen	Sinoffe	Roscommon	Noemia	Sent to service in Rimouski
445	BRENNAN, Mary	?	04/01/48	?	?	?	?	?	Fran. Baudet Lotbinière
242	BRIEN, Ellen	15	09/07/47	John	Margt. Brien	Mondaniel	Cork	Avon	Mr. Boulanger* St. Nicolas thence to Valcartier
243	BRIEN, Patrick	14	09/07/47	John	Margt. Brien	Mondaniel	Cork	Avon	Martin Moylan (Valcartier)
430a	BRIEN, Patrick	14	12/20/47	John	Margt. Brien	*child was returned by adopter			Mr. Maguire, 61 St. Louis thence to Valcartier
244	BRIEN, William	12	09/07/47	John	Margt. Brien	Mondaniel	Cork	Avon	J. Paul Beaubien Nicolet
319	BROOTHER, Anne	6	09/16/47	?		?	?	?	Hilaire Trudelle* St-Hilaire
318	BROTHER, Pat	8	09/16/47	?		?	?	?	Isaie Blackburn Malbaie
442e	BROOTHER, Pat	8	03/09/48	?		* child was returned by adopter			Dominick Henderson rue des Jardins
448	BROWN, Mary	12	04/06/48	Andry	Mary Till	?	Waterford	Thistle	Pierre Tanguay Pte Lévis
455	BROWN, Sarah	20 months	06/48	James	Margt. Steel	?	?	?	Thence to Pierre Boutillette de St-Henri Died Aug. 5
12	BULGER, Patrick	8	07/47	?	?	?	?	?	Returned to parents
449	BURKE, ?	?	04/25/48	?	?	?	?	?	Returned to parents
450	BURKE, ?	?	04/25/48	?	?	?	?	?	Returned to parents
451	BURKE, ?	?	04/25/48	?	?	?	?	?	Returned to parents

No.	Name	Age	Date	Father	Mother	Parish	County	Ship	Notes
333	BURKE, John	11	09/29/47	Thomas	Biddy Haynes	Old Moore	Galway	Champion	Person in Rimouski
307	BURNS, Mary Anne	9	09/20/47	Michael	Mary Healy	Callray	Sligo	Columbia	J.B. Trudelle St. Grégoire thence to Sisters of Charity
305	BURNS, Owen	15	09/20/47	Michael	Mary Healy	Callray	Sligo	Columbia	Mrs. James Finnigan Lower Town
306	BURNS, Thomas	12	09/20/47	Michael	Mary Healy	Callray	Sligo	Columbia	Ambroise Therrien St. Grégoire (clerk in Mtl)
52	BYRNE, Edward	12	07/47	?	?	?	?	?	Died Aug. 5
283	BYRNE, Dennis	6	09/14/47	Dennis	?	?	Roscommon	John Munn	Died Oct. 20
116	BYRNES, Dennis	8	08/14/47	Dennis	Biddy Brown	?	?	Pandora	Francis Gallagher* rue La Montagne
459k	BYRNES, Dennis	8	07/02/48	Dennis	Biddy Brown	* child was returned by adopter			Charles Bouchard Pte Lévis / Father is in Montreal
51	BYRNE, Margaret	10	07/47	?	?	?	?	?	Disappeared
135	BYRNES, Andrew	18	08/18/47	Andrew	Mary Burn	Gilthristle	Boscommon	?	Peter Brady Valcartier
136	BYRNES, Mary	16	08/18/47	?	?	?	?	?	Pat Wheeler* Frampton
432c	BYRNE, Mary	16	12/21/47	?	?	* She returned due to illness			Left for Baltimore to her brother
54	CAHILL, William	12	07/47	?	?	?	?	?	Hugh Gavins Upper Town
346	CAIRNS, Mary	8	10/05/47	Nicholas	Mary Dempsey	Bohola	Mayo	Argyle	Joseph Bouliane le gros Malbaie
345	CAIRNS, Pat	20	10/05/47	Nicholas	Mary Dempsey	Bohola	Mayo	Argyle	Died or left
24	CALLAGHAN, John	10	07/47	?	?	?	?	?	Died Aug. 4
25	CALLAGHAN, Michael	7	07/47	?	?	?	?	?	Died Sept. 20
23	CALLAGHAN, Patrick	12	07/47	?	?	?	?	?	?
339	CAMPBELL, Bridget	14	10/04/47	Thomas	Jane Monahan	Drumcondry	Meath	Greenock	Mrs. Laliberté Lotbinière
338	CAMPBELL, Mary	17	10/04/47	Thomas	Jane Monahan	Drumcondry	Meath	Greenock	Dr. Grenier Lotbinière
261	CAMPBELL, Michael	7	09/07/47	William	Mary Follene	Lisanuffy	Roscommon	Virginias	Bridget Lyng St John Sheet
268	CAMPBELL, Nancy	16	09/07/47	Darbey	Biddy Sheeran	Lisanuffy	Roscommon	Virginias	?
387	CANAHAN, Mary	16	10/17/47	Hugh	Honorah Kildare	?	Clare	Odessa	Left for Clintonville
163	CANAHAN, Thomas	10	08/21/47	Hugh	Honorah Kildare	?	Clare	Odessa	Left for Clintonville
126	CARNAC, John	6	08/14/47	?	?	?	?	?	L'Asile de Québec / Claimed by Lord Bishop of Montréal
426	CARROLL, Mathew	7	12/17/47	?	?	Clonakilty	Cork	Bee	Sent to his uncle by Bishop of Pittsburgh

119

ÉTÉ 1847 / SUMMER OF 1847

No. Rég. Reg. No.	Nom Name	Âge Age	Date d'entrée Date of Entry	Père Father	Mère Mother	Paroisse Parish	Comté County	Bateau Vessel	Adopté par Adopted by
272	CASSIDY, Biddy	8	09/07/47	Edward	Ellen Connor	Rothangan	Kildare	Lady Campbell	Died Oct. 16
273	CASSIDY, Cristopher	7	09/07/47	Edward	Ellen Connor	Rothangan	Kildare	Lady Campbell	Died Oct. 3
274	CASSIDY, Thomas	14	09/07/47	Edward	Ellen Connor	Rothangan	Kildare	Lady Campbell	Mr. P. Villers Lotbinière
185	CAUL, James	10	08/25/47	John	Elizabeth Carroll	Templemore	Derry	Marchioness of Abercorn	Left for St. Catherine
130	CAUL, John	4	08/16/47	John	Elizabeth Carroll	Templemore	Derry	Marchioness of Abercorn	Mary Murphy Valcartier
131	CAUL, Richard	3	08/16/47	John	Elizabeth Carroll	Templemore	Derry	Marchioness of Abercorn	Died — Parents living
459	CAVAGAN, Peter	10	07/02/47	Peter Morris	Mary Clarme	?	?	?	Pierre Langis (Rimouski) Person in St. Basile St Latourelle
458	CAVANAGH, ?	11	05/30/48		Mary Fleming	?	Kilkenny	?	
117	CAVANAGH, Mary	14	08/14/47	?	?	?	?	?	Patrick Fitzsimmons Faubourg St-Jean
335	CAWLY, Hugh	12	10/03/47	Hugh	Peggy Cawly (Cawsly?)	Tipperary	Tipperary	Sir R. Peel	Mr. Wheeler Frampton (his mother is in hosp.)
133	CLARKE, Mary	14	08/16/47	?	?	?	?		Telesphore Methot St-Croix
74	CLOYNE, John	14	08/03/47	?	?	?	?	?	Henry O'Connor grocer St John St.
248	CLYNE, Pat	6	09/07/47	?	?	?	?	?	
36	COLLINS, Margaret	6	07/47	?	?	?	?	?	Died Aug. 3
37	COLLINS, Patrick	5	07/47	?	?	?	?	?	Died Aug. 10
43	CONNELLY, Anne	5	07/47	?	?	?	?	?	Disappeared
41	CONNERS, John	4	07/47	?	?	?	?	?	?
436	CONNOLLY, Bridget	10	02/23/48	Edward	Mary Hynes	Termonamongan	Tyrone	Helen Thompson	Left for St. Pascal
434	CONNOLLY, John	9	02/06/48	Edward	Mary Hynes	Termonamongan	Tyrone	Helen Thompson	Left for St. Pascal
437	CONNOLLY, Mary	7	02/23/48	Edward	Mary Hynes	Termonamongan	Tyrone	Helen Thompson	Left May 26
433	CONNOLLY, Patrick	11	02/06/48	Edward	Mary Hynes	Termonamongan	Tyrone	Helen Thompson	Left May 26 frs St Paschal.
294	CONNOR, Catherine	8	09/20/47	Patrick	Bridget Sweeney	Ballyna	Mayo	Marchioness of Breadalbane	Alex Rivard of Rimouski

No.	Name	Age	Date	Father	Mother	Townland	County	Ship	Notes
293	CONNOR, Mary	12	09/20/47	Patrick	Bridget Sweeney	Ballyna	Mayo	Marchioness of Breadalbane	Fran. Lemieux (Rimouski)
295	CONNOR, Patrick	6	09/20/47	Patrick	Bridget Sweeney	Ballyna	Mayo	Marchioness of Breadalbane	Died Nov. 2
377	CONNORS, James	14	10/06/47	James	Julia Reardon	Kilfinnane	Limerick	Jane Black	Went into service Mother is in hospital in Boston
415	CONORS, Mary	5	11/16/47	James	Julia Reardon	Kilfinnane	Limerick	Jane Black	Left with James fur brother
454	CONNORS, William	2	05/01/48	Thomas	Bridget Connors	?	?	?	Died May 28 — his father lives at Près de Ville
121	CONRAY, Anne	14	08/04/47	Bernard	Catherine Scott	Ballyglass	Roscommon	Georgiana	Thomas Durette Rimouski
122	CONRAY, Bryan	12	08/14/47	Bernard	Catherine Scott	Ballyglass	Roscommon	Georgiana	Pascal Martin Rimouski
210	CONROY, Mary	17	08/30/47	James	Judith Dunn	Clonaslee	Queens	Greenock	Mr. Tachereau Ste. Marie
208	COONEY, John	10	08/30/47	Michael	Catherine Dunn	Bellavrough	Cavan	Phoenix	Remi Noel Ste Croix
296	COUSINS, John	6	09/20/47	Michael	Catherine Cousins	New Ross	Kilkenny	Colonist	M. le Curé St. Grégoire In 1863 got land in St. Wenceslas
30	COX, Anne	5	07/47	?	?	?	?	?	Mr. Gauvreau (Ste Luce)
212	COX, George	9	08/30/47	Martin	Mary Maloney	Bumbleim Bumbline	Roscommon	Virginius	?
211	COX, Mary	7	08/30/47	Martin	Mary Maloney	Bumbleim	Roscommon	Virginius	Mr. Gauvreau (Ste Luce)
256	CHANNY, Michael	5	09/07/47	Thomas	Nancy Toul	?	?	Lady Campbell	?
125	CROWLEY, John	4	08/14/47	?	?	?	?	?	Died Sept. 28
341	CULLEN, Margaret	16	10/04/47	James	Betty Kinny	Logorre	Armagh	Sr. Campbell	Mr. Darveau Faubourg St. Jean
224	CUMMINS, Michael	14	09/02/47	John	Mary Cullen	?	Queens	Lady Campbell	James Masterson Shipton
207	CUNNINGHAM, Margt	13	08/30/47	?	Marg. Shaughnessy	?	?	?	Died Nov. 21 John Brown Lake Beauport
127	CUTTER, John	15	08/14/47	Richard	Onah Tierney	Ricormic	Cork	Avon	Jos Marcheterre Rimouski
129	DALTON, Andrew	13	08/14/47	William	Onah Tierney	Bumblein	Roscommon	Brin's Queen	Pierre Côté Rimouski
298	DALTON, John	5	09/20/47	William	Onah Tierney	Bumblein	Roscommon	Erin's Queen	Thomas Lamen (Lannen?) Cap Blanc
31	DALTON, Michael	6	07/47	William	Onah Tierney	Bumblein	Roscommon	Erin's Queen	

ÉTÉ 1847 / SUMMER OF 1847

No. Rég. Reg. No.	Nom Name	Âge Age	Date d'entrée Date of Entry	Père Father	Mère Mother	Paroisse Parish	Comté County	Bateau Vessel	Adopté par Adopted by
297	DALTON, Suzan	16	09/20/47	William	Onah Tierney	Bumblein	Roscommon	Erin's Queen	Pierre Côté Rimouski
239	DALY, Johanna	6	09/08/47	Owen	Mary Mauntlet	?	Waterford	?	Died Sept. 29 — father in town — mother in hospital
209	DALY, John	11	08/30/47	?	?	?	?	?	Died Sept. 15 Father in U.S.
392	DALY, John	14	10/18/47	Thomas	Margt. Ryan	Gillin	Kings	John Munn	Person in Nicolet
18	DALEY, Margaret	10	07/47	?	?	?	?	?	Walter Shallow Mount Pleasant
20	DALEY, Mary	8	07/47	?	?	?	?	?	Mrs. Elliot Spencer Cove
17	DALEY, Michael	12	07/47	Michael	Mary Walsh	Kilbany	Limerick	Avon	Fran. Morin Nicolet
70	DALY, Norry	15 months	08/02/47	?	?	?	?	?	Mrs. J. Bertrand 50 Richelieu Faubourg St. Jean
19	DALEY, Patrick	6	07/47	?	?	?	?	?	Louis Beaulorier Nicolet
284	DAVY, Thomas M. Ann Walsh in 1860	10	09/14/47	Matthew	Ellen Grady	Newbridge	Kildare	Ganges	Étienne Thibodeau St. Grégoire
14	DAWSON, Patrick	5	07/47	William	?	?	?	?	Left Sept. 11
291	DEEGEN, Bridget	13	09/16/47	Michael	Mary Dwyre	New Ross	Carlow	Progres	Nor. Bellerose of Nicolet M. her benefactor
90	DEMPSEY, Anne	6	08/06/47	Bryan D.	Mary Queen	Boldkell	Kildare	Lady Campbell	Died Aug. 16
91	DEMPSEY, Bridget	4	08/06/47	Bryan D.	Mary Queen	Boldkell	Kildare	Lady Campbell	Died Aug. 23
88	DEMPSEY, Eliza	10	08/06/47	Bryan D.	Mary Queen	Boldkell	Kildare	Lady Campbell	Miss A. Rivard Rimouski
87	DEMPSEY, Hannah	11	08/06/47	Bryan D.	Mary Queen	Boldkell	Kildare	Lady Campbell	J.B. L'Allemand Rimouski
89	DEMPSEY, Mary	9	08/06/47	Bryan D.	Mary Queen	Boldkell	Kildare	Lady Campbell	Miss Marie Gace Rimouski
379	DESMOND, Catherine	18	10/06/17	Mary Sullivan	Kilcolemary	Limerick	Ajax	Entered service Lowertown	
164	DIGNAM, Catherine	13	08/21/47	?	?	?	?	?	R. Flinn Sous-le-fort St.
336	DONOHOE, John	13	10/03/47	John	Catherine Roe	Arins	Wexford	John Bell	C. Gariepy Ste Anne de la Pérade

No.	Name	Age	Date	Father	Mother	Townland	County	Ship	Notes
337	DONOHOE, Mogue	8	10/03/47	John	Catherine Roe	Arins	Wexford	John Bell	L. Dolbec / Ste. Anne de la Pérade
64	DONOVAN, John	5	07/47	?	?	?	?	?	Died Aug. 26
330	DONOVAN, Pat	15	09/29/47	Patrick	Johanna McCarthy	Caree	Cork	Henriette Mary	Mr. Donohue
407	DORION, William	8	10/26/47	Daniel	Cicily Dorion	?	(mother is in Ireland)	Rankin	Champlain Sheet / Person in Rimouski
93	DORNION, Daniel	6	08/06/47	Michael	Catherine Love	Fannoth	Armagh / Donegal	Rankin	Rev. Mr. Faucher / Lotbinière
101	DORSAY, Mary	14	08/09/47	?	?	?	?	?	Died Aug. 22
353	DOWLY, Margaret	10	10/06/47	John	Margaret Nellis	Kellisha	?	22 / Superior	Died Oct. 28 / Mother is in States
331	DOYLE, Lawrence	12	08/29/47	Lawrence	Mary Flinn	Glinnigal	Carlow	Industry	Mr. Lemieux / St. Roch
115	DUFFEY, Mary	7	08/14/47	?	?	?	?	?	Died Sept. 29
446	DUNN, Margaret	14	04/06/48	John	Judith Gaffny	Dorah	Queens	Juverna	Mrs. Ferguson / St. John Street
309	EGAN, Bridget	6	09/20/47	Bryan	Bridget Casy	Hillglass	Roscommon	Erin's Queen	Died Feb. 3, 1848
308	EGAN, Peter	16	09/20/47	Bryan	Bridget Casy	Hillglass	Roscommon	Erin's Queen	Agapit Belanger / Rimouski
255	EGAN, Thomas	6	09/07/47	John	Catherine Kelly	Elphin	Roscommon	Triton	?
7	EVANS, Margaret	15	07/27/47	?	?	?	?	?	Died Aug. 3
32	FAUGHEY, Catherine	10	07/47	?	?	?	?	?	Died Aug. 4
222a	FEENEY, ANNE	8	09/02/47	Thomas	Mary Lyons	Bumblin	Roscommon	Virginius	Mr. Kelly / St. Sylvester
222	FEENEY, Catherine	18	09/02/47	Thomas	Mary Lyons	Bumblin	Roscommon	Virginius	Mr. Kelly / St. Sylvester
249	FEENY, Catherine	14	09/07/47	Michael	Ellen Kelly	Bumblin	Roscommon	Naomi	Died Oct. 1
82	FINNERTY, Hannah	14	08/06/47	Patrick	Catherine Coffy	Foghany	Galway	Blonde	Died Oct. 7 / Brother is in Montreal
334	FITZGERALD, John	10	09/29/47	Edward	Catherine Lehey	?	Kerry	Bridgetown	Jean Bouvette / St. Grégoire
5	FITZPATRICK, Anne	13	07/47	Patrick	Mary Forestal	the Rower	Kilkenny	Progress	Norbert Beliveau / St. Grégoire
99	FITZPATRICK, Bridget	18	08/09/47	Patrick	Mary Forestal	the Rower	Kilkenny	Progress	Jean Prince / St. Grégoire
6	FITZPATRICK, Edward	15	07/47	Patrick	Mary Forestal	the Rower	Kilkenny	Progress	Returned to mother / St. Grégoire
458i	FITZPATRICK, Ellen	8	07/01/48	Patrick	Mary Forestal	the Rower	Kilkenny	?	?
111	FITZPATRICK, Michael	14	08/12/47	?	?	?	?	?	Died Aug. 23
184	FLYNN, Anne	11	08/25/47	John	Onah Bradley	near Rovishtown	Sligo	Wanderer	Died Sept. 30
187	FLYNN, Bridget	2½	08/27/47	John	Onah Bradley	near Rovishtown	Sligo	Wanderer	Died Sept. 24
186	FLYNN, Margaret	13	08/27/47	John	Onah Bradley	near Rovishtown	Sligo	Wanderer	Died Sept. 30

123

ÉTÉ 1847 / SUMMER OF 1847

No. Rég. Reg. No.	Nom Name	Âge Age	Date d'entrée Date of Entry	Père Father	Mère Mother	Paroisse Parish	Comté County	Bateau Vessel	Adopté par Adopted by
250	FOLLEN, Ann	8	09/07/47	John	Kitty Madden	Lesanoffy	Roscommon	?	Disappeared
3456	FOLEY, Mary	5	07/47	?	?	?	Virginius	?	Mrs. Desaulniers
389	FORD, James	4 months	10/18/47	?	Mary Stanly	?	?	?	Three Rivers
340	FORTUNE, Margt.	19	10/04/47	William	Betty Loane	Newrose	Kilkenny	Progress	Person in La Malbaie
197	FOX, Anne	10	08/28/47	Thomas	Mary Carroll	Athlone	Westmeath	Bridgetown	Fran. Couture St. Gervais
198	FOX, Betsey	2	08/28/47	Thomas	Mary Carroll	Athlone	Westmeath	Bridgetown	Died
124	FOX, Catherine	4	08/14/47	?	?	?	?	?	?
200	FOX, Catherine	9	08/28/47	Thomas	Mary Carroll	Athlone	Westmeath	Bridgetown	Died
57	FOX, Margaret	?	07/47	?	?	?	?	?	Died Aug. 9
55	FOX, Patrick	6	07/47	?	?	?	?	?	Died Aug. 9
56	FOX, Peter	8	07/47	?	?	?	?	?	Died Aug. 9
196	FOX, Peter	16	08/28/47	Thomas	Mary Carroll	Athlone	Westmeath	Bridgetown	Mr. Bigaouette St. Gervais
398	GIBSON, Agnes	90	10/22/47	Samuel	Nancy	?	?	?	Reunited with parents Brother in hospital
399	GIBSON, Mary Jane	6	10/22/47	Samuel	Nancy	?	?	?	Reunited with parents
176	GILL, Catherine	13	08/24/47	John	Mary Lynch	Old Castle	Meath	Lady Anne	René Desruisseaux Lotbinière
178	GILL, Henry	9	08/24/47	John	Mary Lynch	Old Castle	Meath	Lady Anne	Died in Lotbinière
177	GILL, Patrick	12	08/24/47	John	Mary Lynch	Old Castle	Meath	Lady Anne	Ambroise Auger Lotbinière
359	GORMOLLY, Arthur (Gormley?)	7	10/06/47	Fergus	Mary Nellis	Killer	Tyrone	Superior	Mrs. Daly Upper Canada
360	GORMOLLY, Mary	5	10/0647	Fergus	Mary Nellis	Killer	Tyrone	Superior	Mrs. Daly Upper Canada
358	GORMOLLY, Mary	5	10/0647	Fergus	Mary Nellis	Killer	Tyrone	Superior	Mrs. Daly Upper Canada
406	GRANT, Edouard	14	10/26/47	John	Peggy Shea	Cussicommon	Kilkenny	Wandsworth	Mr. Rigney Riv.-du-Loup
405	GRIFFIN, Daniel	15	10/26/47	Marc	Mary Lucky	Kill	Meath	Wave	Daniel Fawly St. Casimir
128	HANLY, Michael	10	08/14/47	Edward	Mary Eagan	Thriston	Roscommon	Virginius	Olivier Danneau Nicolet, d. in US 1860
458h	HANLEY, Michael	12	05/20 /48	Edward	Mary Eagan	Thriston	Roscommon	Virginius	Germain Langis Rimouski
142	HANLY, Patrick	13	08/18/47	Phelan	Mary Carroll	Gilthristle	Roscommon	Virginius	?

No.	Name	Age	Date	Father	Mother	Town/Parish	County	Ship	Notes
374	HANNON, Ellen	6	10/06/47	?	?	?	?	?	Died Oct. 26
375	HANNON, Maria	5	10/06/47	?	?	?	?	?	Died Oct. 28
373	HARROWAY, ?	3	10/06/47	?	?	?	?	?	Died at Ile-aux-Coudres Vital Boudreau Ile-aux-Coudres
372	HARROWAY, ?	5	10/06/47	?	?	?	?	?	Ile-aux-Coudres
376	HAWKY, Catherine	9	10/06/47	John	Bridget Kelly	?	Donegal	Countess of Erin	Person in Nicolet
386	HAWKY, Jane	12	10/17/47	John	Bridget Kelly	?	Donegal	Countess of Erin	Sister is in hospital Person in Nicolet
440	HEALY, James	14	02/27/48	?	?	?	?	?	Jean Barbeau Laval
69	HEALEY, James	14	08/02/47	?	?	?	?	?	Rev. W. McKie (Mackie?)
21	HEALEY, James	12	07/47	?	?	?	?	?	Left Aug. 2
22	HEALEY, Mary	10	07/47	?	?	?	?	?	Died Aug. 18
385	HEIK, Emma	20	10/15/47	James	Jane Kane	?	Armagh	Conqueror	Left Oct. 24 – m. old Corrigan, doorkeeper at Marine Hospital. Died in 1862 at Hôtel Dieu
77	HENRY, Daniel (Heney)	12	08/04/47	John	Suzan Murphy	Rocketwist	Tyrone	Larch	Hippolyte Noel Lotbinière
80	HENRY, Francis (Heney)	4	08/04/47	?	?	?	?	?	Died Aug. 31
79	HENRY, James (Heney)	6	08/04/47	John	Suzan Murphy	Rocketwist	Tyrone	Larch	Louis Leclerc Lotbinière
81	HENRY, Susan (Heney)	1	08/04/47	?	?	?	?	?	Died
78	HENRY, William (Heney)	8	08/04/47	John	Suzan Murphy	Rocketwist	Tyrone	Larch	Louis Leclerc Lotbinière
72	HOGAN, Patrick	14	08/03/47	Thomas	Mary Hogan	?	Kildare	John Jordon	James Mangan Champlain St.
162	HOLDEN, Bridget	14	08/20/47	Henry	Bridget Maham	Strokestown	Roscommon	Naomi	Aug. Lavoie dit Samson Rimouski
145	HOLDEN, Henry	9	08/18/47	Henry	Bridget Maham	Strokestown	Roscommon	Naomi	Aug. Lavoie dit Samson Rimouski
144	HOLDEN, John	16	08/18/47	Henry	Bridget Maham	Strokestown	Roscommon	Naomi	Died
146	HOLDEN, Mathew	7	08/18/47	Henry	Bridget Maham	Strokestown	Roscommon	Naomi	Died
278	HOLLAND, Anne	12	09/11/47	Richard	Ann Sullivan	Ballywilliam	?	Mary Anne Harriett	Louis Péruse Lotbinière (mother in Ireland)
38	HOPKINS, Mary	10	07/47	?	?	Medor	Longford	Wandsworth	Her mother – who gave her to Grey Nuns in Montreal
286	HOPPER, John	15	09/15/47	John	Bridget Carrol	Abbeyleix	Queen	Wandsworth	W. Moylan Douglastown
205	HOWARD, Susan	12	08/28/47	?	?	?	?	?	Died Sept. 6
171	HOWLEY, Anne	6	08/22/47	Martin	Catherine Wright	Corbally	Sligo	Larch	Mr. Gaucher Lotbinière

ÉTÉ 1847 / SUMMER OF 1847

No. Rég. Reg. No.	Nom Name	Âge Age	Date d'entrée Date of Entry	Père Father	Mère Mother	Paroisse Parish	Comté County	Bateau Vessel	Adopté par Adopted by
170	HOWLEY, Anne	6	08/22/47	Martin	Catherine Wright	Corbally	Sligo	Larch	Died Sept. 8
11	HUNT, John	2	07/47	?	?	?	?	?	Died Aug. 21
287	HUTCHISON, Courtney	7	09/15/47	Abandoned by parents		?	?	?	Pierre Terrien St Casimir
203	HYLER, Judith (or Hilliard)	14	08/28/47	Andrew	Nancy Fitzpatrick	Hinch	Clare	Champion	Died Sept. 6
202	HYLER, Mary (or Hilliard)	13	08/28/47	Andrew	Nancy Fitzpatrick	Hinch	Clare	Champion	Luc Reau (went 1858 to St. Grégoire Longueuil)
201	HYLER, Michael (or Hilliard)	15	08/28/47	Andrew	Nancy Fitzpatrick	Hinch	Clare	Champion	Louis Beaulorier Nicolet
120	HYNES, Edward	14	08/14/47	James	Mary Hines	Megorna	Mayo	Rankin	Eusège Lepage Rimouski
119	HYNES, Patrick	12	08/14/48	James	Mary Hines	Megorna	Mayo	Rankin	Luc St. Laurent Rimouski
61	IVORY, Catherine	13	07/47	John	Johanna Dunn	O'Harlah	Tipperary	John Francis	G. Thomas dit Bigaouette St. Roch than to Frampton
442f	IVORY, Catherine	13	07/47	John	Johanna Dunn	O'Harlah	Tipperary	John Francis	Michael O'Connor
42	JACKSON, Michael	10	07/47	?	?	?	?	?	John Collins Cap Blanc
213	JAMES, Ann	18	09/02/47	Richard	Judy Neill	Kilguggen	Wicklow	Colonist	Mrs. Méthot Ste. Croix
216	JAMES, Judith	12	09/02/47	Richard	Judy Neill	Kilguggen	Wicklow	Colonist	Mrs. Méthot Ste. Croix
214	JAMES, Larry	16	09/02/47	Richard	Judy Neill	Kilguggen	Wicklow	Colonist	Mr. Boisvert St. Nicolas
217	JAMES, Mary	10	09/02/47	Richard	Judy Neill	Kilguggen	Wicklow	Colonist	Mr. Boisvert St. Nicolas
459L	JAMES, Mary	?	07/02/48	Richard	Judy Neill	Kilguggen	Wicklow	Colonist	William Corcoran
215	JAMES, Patrick	14	09/02/47	Richard	Judy Neill	Kilguggen	Wicklow	Colonist	Mr. Bergeron St. Antoine
1	JENNINGS, John	13	07/27/47	Thad	?	?	?	?	Died Aug. 9
40	JEWELL, Mary	10	07/47	?	?	?	?	?	Mrs. Morisson St. Roch thence to John Venner dry goods
66	JINKS, Bridget	14	07/47	?	?	?	Father living	?	R.P. Levesque Éboulements
323	KANE, Honora	13	09/29/47	John	Bridget McInanly	Newport	Mayo	Sarah	George Lizotte Rimouski
2	KANE, John	9	07/27/47	?	?	?	?	?	Died Aug. 13
324	KANE, Timothy	11	09/29/47	John	Bridget McInanly	Newport	Mayo	Sarah	Hilaire St. Laurent Rimouski

No.	Name	Age	Date	Father	Mother	Townland	County	Ship	Notes
151	KEARIN, Bridget	8	08/18/47	Hugh	Mathilda McPartin	Gilina	Cavan	Ganges	Died
169	KEARIN, Thomas	12	08/21/47	Hugh	Mathilda McPartin	Gilina	Cavan	Ganges	Pat McGauran dry goods 30 Buade
439	KEEGAN, Ellice	4	02/25/48	?	Catherine Gallaher	?	?	?	?
68	KELLY, Catherine	8	08/02/47	Michael	Catherine Gallaher	?	?	?	Widow Is. Sevigné St Antoine
238	KELLY, Ellen	6	09/08/47	Michael	Catherine Gallaher	?	?	?	Hugh Smith* McInenly's Hill
433d	KELLY, Ellen	6	01/27/48	Michael	Catherine Gallaher (Father alive at Marine Hospital)				Jean B. Dubé St-Jean-Port-Joli *child returned by adopter
76	KELLY, Mary	13	08/04/47	David	Mary Walsh	Killaby	Mayo	Anna	Returned to mother in Ohio, to Mr. Bowman, St Roch
348	KENNEDY, Anne	5	10/05/47	John	Margaret Howe	Burris	Tipperary	Sir. R. Peel	Died
384	KENNEDY, Anne	20	10/15/47	Denis	Margaret O'Hara	Kiluren	Clare	Manchester	Left for Boston
227	KENNEDY, Bridget	17	09/04/47	Francis	Mary Kenny	Monaghan	Tipperary	Albion	Returned to parents Quebec
347	KENNEDY, Catherine	12	10/05/47	John	Margaret How	Burris	Tipperary	Sir Robert Peel	Clovis Caron L'Islet
228	KENNEDY, Ellen	20	09/04/47	Francis	Mary Kenny	Monaghan	Tipperary	Albion	In 1854 m. Caron's nephew
352	KENNEDY, Hugh	3	10/06/47	John	Margaret Howe	Burris	Tipperary	Sr. R. Peel	Found her parents
350	KENNEDY, John	9	10/05/47	John	Margaret Howe	Burris	Tipperary	Sr. R. Peel	Died Oct. 24
351	KENNEDY, Michael	7	10/06/47	John	Margaret Howe	Burris	Tipperary	Sr. R. Peel	M. Belanger – sent in 1865 to Asile Canardière; Died Oct. 23
349	KENNEDY, Sylvester	14	10/05/47	John	Margaret Howe	Burris	Tipperary	Sr. R. Peel	Married a widow in Lalendre
267	KENNEDY, Thomas	10	09/07/47	Darbey	Judith Cavanigh	Whitewall	Kilkenny	Bridgetown	Charles Sampson Nicolet
204	KENT, Michael (also 332)	12	08/28/47	Patrick	Judah Hickey	Shandrahan	Tipperary	Trident	Ignace Caron St. Cyril, Islet had a sister at Grosse Ile
143	KILMARTIN, Anne	10	08/18/47	Thomas	Catherine Gaherty	Lissinoufy	Roscommon	Virginius	Jacques Bourgeois St. Grégoire
161	KILMARTIN, Cath.	12	08/20/47	Thomas	Catherine Gaherty	Lissinoufy	Roscommon	Virginius	Died Sept. 5
103	KILBOY, Martin	11	08/11/47	?	?	?	?	?	S. Antoine de Tilly Providence
344	KIRNAN, Margaret	20	10/05/47	Bernard	Biddy McGauran	Drumrily	Leitrim	Superior	Left for Providence
343	KIRNAN, Pat	16	10/05/47	Bernard	Biddy McGauran	Drumrily	Leitrim	Superior	U.S. Nov. 10
240	LARESSY, Pat	10	08/30/47	Phanton	Catherine Daughon	Abbeyleix	Queens	Wandsworth	Mr. Neville
241	LARESSY, Phanton	12	08/30/47	Phanton	Catherine Daughon	Abbeyleix	Queens	Wandsworth	Died Oct. 18
140	LEAHEY, Ellen (had some money)	11	08/18/47	Jacob	Ellen Efferman (Hefferman?)	Bavador	Tipperary	?	Pouliot Pilote Rimouski

ÉTÉ 1847 / SUMMER OF 1847

No. Rég. Reg. No.	Nom Name	Âge Age	Date d'entrée Date of Entry	Père Father	Mère Mother	Paroisse Parish	Comté County	Bateau Vessel	Adopté par Adopted by
141	LEAHEY, Mary	5	08/18/47	?	?	?	?	?	Disappeared
277	LENNON, John	5	09/10/47	Patrick	Mary Collins	Tipperary	Tipperary	?	Returned to father (in hospital)
276	LENNON, Patrick (Lannon)	7	09/10/47	Patrick	Mary Collins	Tipperary	Tipperary	?	Returned to father (in hospital)
275	LENNON, Steven (Lannon)	8	09/10/47	Patrick	Mary Collins	Tipperary	Tipperary	?	Returned to father (in hospital)
156	LEONARD, Anne	14	08/20/47	Nicolas	Mary Carlin	Tullyallen	Louth	Greenock	James Farrell Frampton
157	LEONARD, Catherine	12	08/20/47	Nicolas	Mary Carlin	Tullyallen	Louth	Greenock	Robert Duncan Frampton
158	LEONARD, Judith	9	08/20/47	Nicolas	Mary Carlin	Tullyallen	Louth	Greenock	Died Sept. 7
159	LEONARD, Michael	10	08/20/47	Nicolas	Mary Carlin	Tullyallen	Louth	Greenock	Patrick Farrell Frampton
160	LEONARD, Nicolas	4	08/20/47	Nicolas	Mary Carlin	Tullyallen	Louth	Greenock	Disappeared
60	LESTONE, Matthew	13	07/47	?	?	?	?	?	Patrick McCarthy
223	LYNCH, Bridget	15	09/02/47	Edward	Helen Riley	Egistown	Westmeath	Yorkshire	Pat Boylan Mother in Ireland 5 Dominick St, St Roch Died Oct. 22
289	LYONS, Patrick	6	09/01/47	?	?	?	?	?	had a chest and a bed at Mr Denuete 365 Champlain
48	McALAIR, Catherine	12	07/47	Andrew	Jane Maguire	?	Fermanagh	Rose	Died Sept. 21
47	McALAIR, Mary	10	07/47	Andrew	Jane Maguire	?	Fermanagh	Rose	Jos F. Prince St. Grégoire
417	McATEE, James	10	11/25/47	Michael	Bridget Crourkan	Killivan	Monaghan	Ayrshire	?
416	McATEE, Thomas	14	11/25/47	Michael	Bridget Crourkan	Killivan	Monaghan	Ayrshire	Left Nov 4 for Providence
313	McCABE, Alice	10	09/20/47	Owen	Mary Prior	Drumrily	Leitrim	Superior	Left Nov 4 for Providence
312	McCABE, Mary	14	09/20/47	Owen	Mary Prior	Drumrily	Leitrim	Superior	to 3 brothers-in-law Hugh, Michael, James Coley in Carby
371	McCARTY, Michael	6	10/06/47	Patrick	Margt. McGauran	?	Leitrim	Superior	Person in Nicolet
390	McCAW, James	14	10/18/47	John	Grace McGravy	Ballymory	Antrim	Christiana	John Flanagan St. Elzéar
427	McCULL, Eliza	13	12/17/47	William	Suzan Wafer	Ardamine	Wexford	Royalist	George McDonald grocer 23 St. Paul Quebec Mother took her

128

No.	Name	Age	Date	Father	Mother	Parish	County	Ship	Placement / Notes
190	McDERMOT, Mary	14	08/28/47	Thomas	Mary Cormick	Fillglass	Roscommon	Naomi	David Poiré / St. Nicolas
189	McDERMOT, Thomas	12	08/28/47	Thomas	Mary Cormick	Fillglass	Roscommon	Naomi	Died (had money)
453	McDONNELL, Cath.	6	04/26/48	Bernard	Ann Egan	widowed mother in Près-de-Ville			Jean B. Auger
452	McDONNELL, Mary Jane	10	04/26/48	Bernard	Ann Egan	widowed mother in Près-de-ville			Mrs. Leblond / Faubourg St. Roch
154	McFAGAN, Anne	12	08/20/47	Michael	Mary Kelly	Ballyadam	Queens	Wandsworth	?
155	McFAGAN, John	10	08/20/47	Michael	Mary Kelly	Ballyadam	Queens	Wandsworth	Died Sept. 7
357	McGARRETY, Michael	13	10/06/47	Peter	Judith McManus	Drumrily	Leitrim	Superior	M. McLilly, tailor / St. Anne St.
3	McGARRILL, Cath.	13	07/47	Thadeus	Mary Delary	Drumrily	Cavan	Royalist	Louis Bibault / Lotbinière—went later to New Yk
4	McGARRILL, Nancy	10	07/47	Thadeus	Mary Delary	Drumrily	Cavan	Royalist	J.B. Belanger / Lotbinière
327	McGEE, Anne	15	09/29/47	Torry	Mary Owens	Covemenagh	Fermanagh	Rose	François Hamel / Parents are in Ireland / Lotbinière
288	McGILL, Alex	4	09/15/47	?	?	?	?	?	Alexis Bolduc / St. Isidore
457	McGILL, James	8	06/09/48	Bernard	child born in Quebec				Jean B. Beaulieu / St-Arsène, Rimouski
174	McGINNIS, Peter	20 months	08/23/47	?	has a brother Patrick (17) Sr. Jane Eliza (15)—reported by latter in 1851 / mother is a nurse in the hospital				Nicolas Boucher / Lotbinière
409	McGINTY, Jon	4	11/14/47	John	Peggy Huly	?	England	?	Zacharie Perron / Ile aux Coudres
285	McGOMMERIE, James (Montgomery?)	5	09/04/47	?	?	?	?	?	?
29	McGOWEN, James (McGovern)	14	07/47	?	?	?	?	?	R.P.T. Levesque / Malbaie
442	McGRATH, Jane	7	03/09/48	?	?	?	?	?	Francis Martin* / Valcartier
?	McGRATH, Jane	?	?	Returned and was given to Mrs. Ant. Fortier on August 24, 1848					
44	McGRATH, Margaret had money at Moylan's	6	07/47	John	Mary Sullivan	Galbally	Limerick	?	Mrs. George Devlin / Pointe Lévis
281	McGRATH, Mary Anne	6	09/14/47	Michael	Anne McGrath	—under name of Wilson married Arseneau of St. Grégoire			Louis Caillé / St. Grégoire
46	McGRATH, Michael	4	07/47	money at Moylan's		?	?	?	John Collins / Champlain Street
45	McGRATH, Owen	8	07/47	money at Moylan's		?	?	?	Mrs. George Devlin / Pointe Lévis
280	McGRATH, William	7	09/14/47	Michael	Anne McGrath	?	?	?	Paul Bro / St. Grégoire

No. Rég. / Reg. No.	Nom / Name	Âge / Age	Date d'entrée / Date of Entry	Père / Father	Mère / Mother	Paroisse / Parish	Comté / County	Bateau / Vessel	Adopté par / Adopted by
123	McGUIRE, Michael	13	08/14/47	?	?	?	?	?	Died Aug. 27
438	McKENNEY, James	12	02/23/48	?	?	?	?	?	Mr. Lahaie Lotbinièrfe
328	McKILLAN, Bernard	13	09/29/47	Bernard abandoned by parents	May Devlin	Dunhein	Antrim	Tamarac	Ambroise Lemay Lotbinière
329	McKILLAN, Rose	12	09/29/47	Bernard abandoned by parents	May Devlin	Dunhein	Antrim	Tamarac	H. Leclerc Lotbinière
188	McKIRNAN, Bridget	9	08/28/47	Steven	Aby McGirnan	?	Derone Tyrone?	Lady Seaton	
421	McMANUS, John	11	12/07/47	Hugh	Catherine Skey	?	Tyrone	?	Mr. Spencer Riv.-du-Loup
397	McMANUS, Pat	8	10/22/47	Hugh	Catherine Skey	?	Tyrone	?	Mr. Kelly Riv.-du-Loup
147	McNEIL, Michael	13	08/18/47	?	?	?	?	?	Died beginning of Sept.
94	McNICHOLAS, Bridget	10	08/06/47	Pat	Mary Melliham	Twinsworth (Swinsworth)	Mayo	Brougham	?
100	McNICHOLAS, Jane	20	08/09/47	Pat	Mary Melliham	Twinsworth (Swinsworth)	Mayo	Brougham	Mrs. Francis Martin Valcartier, thence to U.S.
95	McNICHOLAS, Mary	9	08/06/47	Pat	Mary Melliham	Twinsworth	Mayo	Brougham	Died Aug. 20
96	McNICHOLAS, Robert	3	08/06/47	Pat	Mary Melliham	Twinsworth	Mayo	Brougham	Died Aug. 31
395	McRAE, Anne	10	10/18/47	Farre	Margaret	?	Loughelsh	Eliza	Notary Lebel Carleton then to U.S.
394	McRAE, Ellen	12	10/18/47	Farre	Margaret	?	Loughelsh	Eliza	Parent family Rimouski
454g	McREAVY, Ann	10	05/26/48	Michael	Margaret McGuire	Glennoly	Fermanagh	?	Mrs. Henny St. Joseph St in Ste Catherine
279	McREAVY, Sarah	14	09/14/47	Michael	Margaret McGuire	Glennoly	Fermanagh	Pursuit	William Hopkins St. Sylvester
63	McVEY, James	12	07/47	Pat	Mary Rafferty	Cappagh	Tyrone	Lord Seaton	Telesphore Roy St.-Jean-Port-Joli
149	MADDEN, Maria	11	08/18/47	James	Mary Kenny	Lissinoufy	Roscommon	Virginius	John Flanagan Stoneham
148	MADDEN, Patrick	17	08/18/47	James	Mary Kenny	Lissinoufy	Roscommon	Virginius	John Flanagan Stoneham
252	MAHON, Catherine	8	09/07/47	James	Ann Clancy	?	Leitrim	Sesostris	Fran, Morin Nicolet
363	MAHON, James	8	10/06/47	John	Ellen Mahon	Riseisver	Leitrim	Argo	Left Oct 28 Toronto for their father John
362	MAHON, John	12	10/06/47	John	Ellen Mahon	Riseisver	Leitrim	Argo	Left Oct 28 Toronto to father John

No.	Name	Age	Date	Father	Mother	Townland	County	Ship	Notes
365	MAHON, Margaret	14	10/06/47	John	Ellen Mahon	Riseisver	Leitrim	Argo	Left Oct 28 Toronto to father John
8	MAHON, Pat	14	07/47	James	Ann Clancy	?	Leitrim	Sesostris	M. Lecomte Nicolet
361	MAHON, Terry	10	10/06/47	John	Ellen Mahon	Riseisver	Leitrim	Argo	Left Oct 28 Toronto to father John
361	MAHON, Thomas	5	10/06/47	John	Ellen Mahon	Riseisver	Leitrim	Argo	Died Oct. 23
264	MAHONEY, Maurice	9	09/07/47	David	Ellen Cashman	Cornavor	Cork	Asia	?
423	MALON, John	14	12/14/47	Charles	Margaret McVey	Dundale	Louth	Wellington	Michael Henchy St. Catherine
410	MILLIGAN, John	16	11/14/47	John	Judah Dowlan	Casteltar	Cavan	Greenock	Left Nov. 20
206	MANAHAN, William	3	08/28/47	?	?	?	?	?	Mary Jane Falls at Mr. Jones, Canardière
383	MOONAN, Margaret	5	10/09/47	?	?	?	?	?	Vital Boudreau Ile-aux-Coudres
382	MOONAN, Mary	7	10/09/47	?	?	?	?	?	Died Oct. 23
132	MOONEY, Anne	5	08/16/47	?	?	?	?	?	Died Sept. 1
71	MOONEY, Bridget	?	08/02/47	?	?	?	?	?	Died
65	MOONEY, Bridget	9	07/47	?	?	?	?	?	James Mahon St. François, St. Uppertown
67	MOONEY, John	5	07/47	?	?	?	?	?	Died Aug. 6
444	MOONEY, Lawrence	15	04/01/48	?	?	?	?	?	Edward Finlay Valcartier
15	MOORE, Patrick	14	07/47	James	?	?	?	?	Left hospital Sept 29 J.B. Corriveau Rimouski
92	MORIARTY, Ellen	14	08/06/47	James	Judith Gallivan	?	?	?	Person in Rimouski
388	MORISSON, Pat	6	10/17/47	James	Bridget	?	Fermanagh	Henry	sent to St. Jean Port Joli Feb 22 1848 mother in hospital
403	MULHERN, Ellen	13	10/23/47	John	Margaret McGauran	?	Fermanagh	Henry	Germain Belanger St-Jean-Port-Joli
424	MULHERN, Margaret	12	12/15/47	John	Margaret McGauran	?	Fermanagh	Henry	sent to St. Jean Port Joli Feb 22 1848
404	MULHERN, Mary	2	10/23/47	John	Margaret McGauran	?	Fermanagh	Henry	sent to St. Jean Port Joli Feb 22 1848
402	MULHERN, Pat	7	10/23/47	John	Margaret McGauran	?	Fermanagh	Henry	sent to St. Jean Port Joli Feb 22 1848
104	MURPHY, Anne	3	08/11/47	?	Ellen Whelan	Ardamine	?	?	Returned to mother
9	MURPHY, Edward	15 months	07/47	John	Mary Curn	?	Wexford	Erin	Died Aug. 10
396	MURPHY, George	13	10/22/47	John	Mary Delaney	Abbeyleix	Wicklow	Agent	Person in Nicolet
265	MURPHY, John	10	09/07/47	Thomas	Anne Murray	Bumblin	Queens	Odessa	?
314	MURPHY, John	12	09/20/47	John	?	?	Rose	Naomi	Left hospital Oct 22 to an uncle in Montreal
75	MURPHY, John	?	08/04/47	?	?	?	?	?	Died Aug. 20
10	MURPHY, Mary	?	/07/47	?	?	?	?	?	Died Aug. 21
266	MURPHY, Michael	7	09/07/47	Thomas	Mary Delaney	Abbeyleix	Queens	Odessa	?

ÉTÉ 1847 / SUMMER OF 1847

No. Rég. / Reg. No.	Nom / Name	Âge / Age	Date d'entrée / Date of Entry	Père / Father	Mère / Mother	Paroisse / Parish	Comté / County	Bateau / Vessel	Adopté par / Adopted by
290	MURPHY, Murdock	7	09/16/47	John	Ellen Whelan	?	?	?	Returned to father Quebec
175	MURRAY, Anne	6	08/23/47	?	?	?	?	?	Died Oct. 30
447	MURRAY, Margaret	14	04/06/48	John	Biddy Murphy	Skreen	Wexford	Marquet	Michael Synnott Wolfe's Cove
181	MURRAY, Maria	11	08/24/47	?	?	?	?	?	Dennis Sheahan 19 Champlain Street
408	NAIL, Anne	13	11/08/47	John	Mary Murphy	Drumkin	Meath	Wandsworth	M. Beaudry Malbaie

This girl has a brother Patrick at Neville's, Valcartier; John at Mme Donney, dyer at Quebec

No. Rég. / Reg. No.	Nom / Name	Âge / Age	Date d'entrée / Date of Entry	Père / Father	Mère / Mother	Paroisse / Parish	Comté / County	Bateau / Vessel	Adopté par / Adopted by
113	NEIL, Thomas	13	08/12/47	?	?	?	?	?	Died Sept. 19
182	NOLAN, Eliza	11	08/25/47	Peter	Mary Cassidy	Strokestown	Roscommon	Bleinheim	Returned to parents
183	NOLAN, John	12	08/25/47	Peter	Mary Cassidy	Strokestown	Roscommon	Bleinheim	Returned to parents
322	NOONAN, Bridget m.a Bergeron at St. Grégoire	11	09/29/47	Patrick	Mary Coleman	Lamon Valley	Westmeath	Odessa	Person in St. Grégoire
321	NOONAN, Cath. m.a Leblanc at Stanfold	20	09/29/47	Patrick	Mary Coleman	Lamon Valley	Westmeath	Odessa	Person in St. Grégoire
304	NOONAN, Margaret Married at St. Christopher	8	09/20/47	Patrick	Mary Coleman	Lamon Valley	Westmeath	Odessa	Isaie Héon St. Grégoire
320	NOONAN, Margaret m. Drulets at St. Grégoire	22	09/29/47	Patrick	Mary Coleman	Lamon Valley	Westmeath	Odessa	Person in St. Grégoire
303	NOONAN, Mary m. her adoptive brother, d. TB 1851	15	09/20/47	Patrick	Mary Coleman	Lamon Valley	Westmeath	Odessa	Fran. Bergeron St. Grégoire
302	NOONAN, Pat	5	09/20/47	Patrick	Mary Coleman	Lamon Valley	Westmeath	Odessa	Louis Leblanc St. Grégoire
460	NOWLAN, Andrew	12	07/14/48	Andrew	Margaret Connors	Capo White	Tipperary	Ganges	Richard Stillman Quebec
431	NOWLAN, Eliza	9	02/04/48	Andrew	Margaret Connors	Capo White	Tipperary	Ganges	Given to their uncle John Connors Shoemaker Champlain St
432	NOWLAN, Grace	7	02/04/48	Andrew	Margaret Connors	Capo White	Tipperary	Ganges	Given to their uncle John Connors
430	NOWLAN, Margaret	15	02/04/48	Andrew	Margaret Connors	Capo White	Tipperary	Ganges	J.B. Martin St. Paschal
118	NUGENT, Catherine	10	08/11/47	John	Sally Nally	Kildare	Roscommon	Naomi	Charles Paquet Rimouski
428	NUNN, Augustus	12	12/17/47	Augustus	Suzan Wafer	Ardamine	Wexford	Royalist	Died Jan 13, 1848
429	NUNN, Letitia	9	12/17/47	Augustus	Suzan Wafer	Ardamine	Wexford	Royalist	Given March 6
16	O'DWYER, Honora	20 months	07/47	?	?	?	?	Progress	Died Aug. 6
86	O'NEIL, Bridget	6	08/06/47	Peter	Mary Hughes	?	Wicklow	Progress	Died

No.	Name	Age	Date	Father	Mother	Parish	County	Ship	Remarks
292	O'NEIL, Catherine	17	09/16/47	Michael	Mary Sheeran	Abbeyleix	Queens	Wandsworth	Mr. Nairne Malbaie
225	O'NEIL, Helen	16	09/04/47	Michael	Mary Sheeran	Abbeyleix	Queens	Wandsworth	Mr. Nairne Malbaie
226	O'NEIL, Mary	18	09/04/47	Michael	Mary Sheeran	Abbeyleix	Queens	Wandsworth	Mr. Nairne Malbaie
85	O'NEIL, Mary Anne	8	08/06/47	Peter	Mary Hughs	?	Wicklow	Progress	Died
84	O'NEIL, Owen	12	08/06/47	Peter	Mary Hughs	?	Wicklow	Progress	Left Aug. 12
83	O'NEIL, Thomas	14	08/06/47	Peter	Mary Hughs	?	Wicklow	Progress	Left Aug. 12
35	PHELAN, Judith	10	07/47	Denis	Catherine Delary	?	Ballynany	Progress	Charles Bergeron St. Grégoire left for service in 1863
180	POWELL, James	4	08/24/47	?	?	?	?	?	Died Sept. 26
179	POWELL, Mary	6	08/24/47	?	?	?	?	?	Died Sept. 5
316	POWER, Margaret	23 days	09/24/47	?	?	?	?	?	Died Sept. 25
299	PRIOR, Andrew	11	09/20/47	Thomas	Margaret McGinis	Drumrily	Leitrim	Superior	Person in Rimouski
300	PRIOR, Catherine	9	09/20/47	Thomas	Margaret McGinis	Drumrily	Leitrim	Superior	Person in Rimouski
301	PRIOR, James	7	09/20/47	Thomas	Margaret McGinis	Drumrily	Leitrim	Superior	Person in Rimouski
	A brother died at Grosse Ile								
412	QUAIL, Catherine	14	11/14/47	Francis	Frances McAlaher	?	Fermanagh	Phoenix	Eugene Sirois St. André
413	QUAIL, Ellen	10	11/14/47	Francis	Frances McAlaher	?	Fermanagh	Phoenix	Michel Chénart Ste. Hélène
411	QUAIL, Francis	15	11/14/47	Francis	Frances McAlaher	?	Fermanagh	Phoenix	Jean M. Carlot St. Paschal
414	QUAIL, Thomas	8	11/14/47	Francis	Frances McAlaher	?	Fermanagh	Phoenix	Hilaire Beaulieu Ste. Hélène
269	QUINN, Pat	12	09/07/47	James	Peggy Lyons	Lisanuffy	Roscommon	Naomi	George Bourke Nicolet
	became a priest in 1862								
270	QUINN, Thomas	6	09/07/47	James	Peggy Lyons	Lisanuffy	Roscommon	Naomi	Rev Hubert Robson sent him to Bourke at Nicolet
	became a priest 1864								
53	REARDON, James	15	07/47	?	?	?	?	?	F. DeVillers Lotbinière
194	REILLEY, Andrew	9	08/28/47	James	Mary Kirmy	New Abbey	Kildare	Bridgetown	Ch. Lavoie dit Samson Rimouski
152	REILLEY, Bridget	7	08/19/47	Thomas	Mary Barry		Roscommon	Avon	Ladies of the Hôpital Général
	m. Aug 1860 to M. Austreul Samson								
192	REILLEY, David	16	08/28/47	James	Mary Kirmy	New Abbey	Kildare	Bridgetown	? Cloutier St. Fabien
317	REILLY, Helena	12	09/28/47	Thomas	Mary Barry	Cork	Roscommon	Avon	Ladies of the Hôpital Général
	became a Religious, biographer of Bishop St-Vallier								
195	REILLEY, James	6	08/28/47	James	Mary Kirmy	New Abbey	Kildare	Bridgetown	Died £14 with Buchanan
193	REILLEY, Mary	14	08/28/47	James	Mary Kirmy	New Abbey	Kildare	Bridgetown	Died Sept. 26 £14 with Buchanan

ÉTÉ 1847 / SUMMER OF 1847

No. Rég. / Reg. No.	Nom / Name	Âge / Age	Date d'entrée / Date of Entry	Père / Father	Mère / Mother	Paroisse / Parish	Comté / County	Bateau / Vessel	Adopté par / Adopted by
153	REILLEY, Mary	5	08/19/47	Thomas	Mary Barry	Cork	Roscommon	Avon	Ladies of the Hôpital Général. Father in hospital
191	REILLEY, Patrick	18	08/28/47	James	Mary Kirmy	New Abbey	Kildare	Bridgetown	Antoine Larouche £14 with Buchanan Rimouski
150	REYNOLDS, Bernard	13	08/18/47	Bernard	Mary Mahon	Gilthristle	Roscommon	?	Left Nov 4 for Baltimore
369	RIELY, Catherine	10	10/06/47	James	Catherine Moore	Tomrasin	Fermanagh	Superior	Herbert Mercier St. Thomas
393	RIELY, Mary	18	10/18/47	James	Catherine Moore	Tomrasin	Fermanagh	Superior	Person in St. Thomas
370	RIELY, Margaret	6	10/06/47	James	Catherine Moore	Tomrasin	Fermanagh	Superior	Person in St. Thomas
367	RIELY, Michael	13	10/06/47	James	Catherine Moore	Tomrasin	Fermanagh	Superior	Dr. Larue Cacouna
368	RIELY, Thomas	8	10/06/47	James	Catherine Moore	Tomrasin	Fermanagh	Superior	Person in St. Thomas
456	ROBINSON, John	12	06/09/48	Thomas	Marie Boucher	Born in Québec			Octave Duchene Rimouski
259	RODRICK, Ann	6	09/07/47	Michael	Honora Burgan	Rathdowny	Queens	Naparima	?
260	RODRICK, Ellen	5½	09/07/47	Michael	Honora Burgan	Rathdowny	Queens	Naparima	Died Sept. 13
257	RODRICK, Mary	11	09/07/47	Michael	Honora Burgan	Rathdowny	Queens	Naparima	?
258	RODRICK, Pat	5	09/07/47	Michael	Honora Burgan	Rathdowny	Queens	Naparima	?
245	ROURKE, Hugh	16	09/07/47	Hugh	Ann Maguire	Curan	Monahand	Coromandel	J.B. Mottard Ste. Croix
366	RYAN, Margaret £1-18	14	10/06/47	Michael	Catherine Hogan	Nockevally	Tipperary	Avon	Left Nov 14 to live with uncle Hogan at Chateauguay, New York State
419	RYAN, Margaret	10	11/25/47	James	Biddy	?	Galway	Thistle	Mrs. Murphy Valcartier
253	RYAN, Mary	14	09/07/47	Edward	Eliza McGauran	Annanduff	Leitrim	John Munn	Died
59	RYAN, Nancy	16	07/47	Michael	Catherine Hogan	Nockevally	Tipperary	Avon	Jonathan Wilkins Cap Blanc
418	RYAN, Patrick	12	11/25/47	James	Biddy	?	Galway	Thistle	Mrs. Murphy Valcartier
420	RYAN, Thomas	8	11/25/47	James	Biddy	?	Galway	Thistle	Died Dec. 24
58	RYAN, Thomas	10	07/47	Michael	Catherine Hogan	Nockevally	Tipperary	Avon	William Breen* Cap Blanc
431b	RYAN, Thomas	10	12/20/47	Michael	Catherine Hogan	* Child was sent to Chateauguay, New York in 1848			
254	RYAN, William	13	09/07/47	Edward	Eliza McGauran	Annanduff	Leitrim	John Munn	Nick Wheeler Frampton
271	SANDERS, Jane	16	09/07/47	James	Rebecca Carson	Clunelochar	Leitrim	Ellen Carr	Prôtestant
168	SCANLON, Anne	7	08/21/47	Patrick	Catherine Kennedy	Macavalley	Tipperary	Anne Kenny	Died Sept. 9

ID	Name	Age	Date	Father	Mother	Townland	County	Ship	Notes
112	SCANLON, Dennis	11	08/12/47	Patrick	Catherine Kennedy	Macavelly	Tipperary	Anne Kenny	Returned to his father
380	SHALOOW, William	14	10/09/47	Dennis	Mary Delany	Ballyadam	Queens	Herald	William Flanagan St Elzéar—sent to St. Helene in 1848
50	SHEAHAN, Mary	13	07/47	James	Mary Fohey	Mundnell	Cork	Avon	Mrs. Crolly Dauphine St. Upper Town
218	SHERIDAN, Ann	15	09/02/47	James	Mary Connor	Lisanuffy	Roscommon	Naomi	Left for Lockport Oct. 2
219	SHERIDAN, Catherine	20	09/02/47	James	Mary Connor	Lisanuffy	Roscommon	Naomi	Left for Lockport Oct. 2
262	SHERIDAN, Ellen	12	09/07/47	James	Mary Connor	Lisanuffy	Roscommon	Naomi	Left for Lockport Oct. 2
220	SHERIDAN, Mary	19	09/02/47	James	Mary Connor	Lisanuffy	Roscommon	Naomi	Left for Lockport Oct. 2
221	SHERIDAN, Owen	14	09/07/47	James	Mary Connor	Lisanuffy	Roscommon	Naomi	Left for Lockport Oct. 2
263	SHERIDAN, Pat	10	09/07/47	James	Mary Connor	Lisanuffy	Roscommon	Naomi	Left for Lockport Oct. 2
49	SHINE, Mary	14	07/47	?	?	?	?	?	Given to her sister
165	SKELTON, ANNE	8	08/21/47	?	?	?	?	?	Sent to her uncle in Shelby, Ohio 06/19/48
167	SHEKELTON, James	5	08/21/47	?	?	?	?	?	Died Sept. 3
166	SKELTON, John	7	08/21/47	?	?	?	?	?	Sent to her uncle inN Shelby, Ohio 06/19/48
173	SKELLY, Patrick	9 months	08/23/47	?	?	?	?	?	Died Aug. 30
315	SLANEY, John	16	09/24/47	Richard	Mary Meade	Capiline	Cork	Lively	Sent to J.B. Dionne in St. Pascal
282	SLANEY, Thomas	8	09/14/47	Richard	Mary Meade	Capiline	Cork	Lively	Mrs. L.A. Desrochers St. Paschal
422	STATRABLE, Ellen	17 months	12/11/47	Thomas	Margaret Pegwell	Glynn	Limerick	Dean of Limerick	Reunited with brother
134	STEWART, Alexander	18	08/18/47	James	Ellen Calaghan	Kildare	Roscommon	Naomi	Louis Richard Stanfold, St. Grégoire
105	SULLIVAN, John	18 months	08/11/47	?	?	?	?	?	Returned to mother
378	SULLIVAN, John	8	10/06/47	John	Johanna	?	?	?	Died Oct. 20
435	SULLIVAN, John	15	02/17/48	John	Bridget Coughlan	Killarney	Kerry	Highland Mary	John Maguire lawyer St. Louis St. Québec
401	SULLIVAN, Thomas	13	10/23/47	Charles	Catherine Sweeny	Schull	Cork	?	Went into service in 11/04/47
137	TIGHE, Catherine	9	08/18/47	Bernard	Mary Kelly	Lissinoufy	Roscommon	Naomi	Fran. Coulombe Lotbinière
138	TIGHE, Daniel	12	08/18/47	Bernard	Mary Kelly	Lissinoufy	Roscommon	Naomi	Fran. Coulombe Lotbinière
33	TIMMONS, Anne	12	07/47	?	?	?	?	?	Died Aug. 2
325	TOOLE, Catherine	15	09/29/47	Frank	Mary Burns	Tilhoy	Kildare	Lady Campbell	Died Oct. 21
326	TOOLE, Ellen	12	09/29/47	Frank	Mary Burns	Tilhoy	Kildare	Lady Campbell	John Hillis Port St. Francis

ÉTÉ 1847 / SUMMER OF 1847

No. Rég. Reg. No.	Nom Name	Âge Age	Date d'entrée Date of Entry	Père Father	Mère Mother	Paroisse Parish	Comté County	Bateau Vessel	Adopté par Adopted by
441	TRAHY, Michael	12	02/09/48	?	?	?	?	?	Dennis Shanahan St. Basile
110	WALL, Michael	12	08/12/47	James	Mary Whelan	Abbeyleix	Queens	Wandsworth	Returned to mother
109	WALL, Patrick	14	08/12/47	James	Mary Whelan	Abbeyleix	Queens	Wandsworth	Returned to mother
246	WARD, Mary	14	09/07/47	Thidy	Sally McGauran	Kilrone	Roscommon	Charles Richard	Fran. Pelletier Nicolet
247	WARD, Rosanna	9	09/07/47	Thidy	Sally McGauran	Kilrone	Roscommon	Charles Richard	Ant. Beauchemin Nicolet
391	WARD, Thomas	15	10/18/47	Thomas	Nancy Goorde	?	Galway	Blonde	Person in Nicolet
425	WATERS, Peter	10	12/15/47	Patrick	Margaret McGowen	Sligo	Sligo	Richard Watson	S. Beaupré, Ecr. St. Pascal
354	WAX, Abbee	11	10/06/47	James	Mary Crostle	Napride	Cavan	Bridgetown	K. Flinn King St, St-Roch
355	WAX, Ellen	10	10/06/47	James	Mary Crostle	Napride	Cavan	Bridgetown	Michel Flinn Dominic St St-Roch
106	WELSH, Bridget	12	09/11/47	?	?	?	?	?	Returned to father
39	WELSH, Mary	6	07/47	?	?	?	?	?	Died Aug. 21
108	WELSH, Patrick	9	08/11/47	Patrick	Honora Joice	Kilmeena	Mayo	Greenock	?
107	WELSH, William	7	08/11/47	?	father died in hospital	?	?	?	Died
98	WHELAN, James	3	08/09/47	Timothy	?	?	?	?	Died
97	WHELAN, Mary	4	08/09/47	Timothy	?	?	?	?	Died Oct. 12
400	WINTER, Mary Anne	6	10/22/47	John	Nancy	?	?	?	Severin Thibault St-Jean-Port-Joli
235	WOODLOCK, Bridget	8	09/08/47	David	Mary Gorman	Goulden	Tipperary	Saguenay	Left to join brothers in Upper Canada
232	WOODLOCK, David	14	09/08/47	David	Mary Gorman	Goulden	Tipperary	Saguenay	Left to join brothers in Upper Canada
233	WOODLOCK, Edward	12	09/08/47	David	Mary Gorman	Goulden	Tipperary	Saguenay	Left to join brothers in Upper Canada
230	WOODLOCK, John	18	09/08/47	David	Mary Gorman	Goulden	Tipperary	Saguenay	Left to join brothers in Upper Canada
236	WOODLOCK, Kate	6	09/08/47	David	Mary Gorman	Goulden	Tipperary	Saguenay	Left to join brothers in Upper Canada
231	WOODLOCK, Margaret	15	09/08/47	David	Mary Gorman	Goulden	Tipperary	Saguenay	Left to join brothers in Upper Canada
234	WOODLOCK, Mary	7	09/08/47	David	Mary Gorman	Goulden	Tipperary	Saguenay	Left to join brothers in Upper Canada
229	WOODLOCK, Thomas	20	09/08/47	David	Mary Gorman	Goulden	Tipperary	Saguenay	Left to join brothers in Upper Canada

ÉTÉ 1848 / SUMMER OF 1848

No. Rég. Reg. No.	Nom Name	Âge Age	Date d'entrée Date of Entry	Père Father	Mère Mother	Paroisse Parish	Comté County	Bateau Vessel	Adopté par Adopted by
560	AGNEW, Edward	2	06/29/48	?	?	?	?	?	Mr. Murphy Champlain St
499	BORLAND, Catherine	13	09/08/48	James	Mary Mitchell	Colhaine	Fermanagh	?	Joseph Hepelle Rimouski
486	BOYLE, Edward	7	06/30/48	Thaddy	Peggy Jennings	Onagh	Galway	St. John	Thomas Walsh Rimouski
485	BOYLE, Thomas	14	06/30/48	Thaddy	Peggy Jennings	Onagh	Galway	St. John	Clement Hins* St. Henry
?	BOYLE, Thomas		08/26/48	Thaddy	Peggy Jennings				Thomas Parent Rimouski
					* Sent to Rimouski on 09/08/48				
461c	BREEN, Johnanne	?	07/02/48	?	?	?	?	?	Mrs. Bedford (aunt) Champlain Street
461a	BREEN, Thomas	?	07/02/48	?	?	?	?	?	Mr. Ballantyne L'Islet
461d	BREEN, ?	?	07/02/48	?	?	?	?	?	Mrs. Moriarity Wolfe's Cove
461b	BREEN, ?	?	07/02/48	?	?	?	?	?	Mr. Giasson L'Islet
540	BRENNAN, John	4	06/22/48	?	?	?	?	?	Mr. Boucher (died) Diamond Harbour
591	BURN, Edward	4	07/48	?	?	?	?	?	Isaie Côté St. Antoine
592	BURN, Lucy	14	07/48	?	?	?	?	?	Louis Côté St. Antoine
588	BURN, Mathew	8	07/48	?	?	?	?	?	Mr. McDonald Upper Canada
564	BYRNES, Margaret	15	06/27/48	?	?	?	?	?	Pierre Hamel
498	CALLAGHAN, Thomas	12	08/17/48	?	?	?	?	Thorny Close	? Dorion Charlesbourg
537	CALLAHAN, John	10	06/22/48	?	?	?	?	Ajax	Pat Water Près-de-Ville
536	CALLAHAN, Margaret	12	06/22/48	?	?	?	?	Ajax	Mr. Kennedy Près-de-Ville
475	CANAHAN, Bridget	12	06/07/48	Patrick	Bridget Shanahan	Arable	Clare	Governor	Louis Fréchette Pointe Lévy
473	CANAHAN, John	8	06/07/48	Patrick	Bridget Shanahan	Arable	Clare	Governor	Joseph Samson Pointe Lévy
476	CANAHAN, Mary	9	06/07/48	Patrick	Bridget Shanahan	Arable	Clare	Governor	Vital Cloutier Pointe Lévy
474	CANAHAN, Michael	16	06/07/48	Patrick	Bridget Shanahan	Arable	Clare	Governor	Pierre Carrier Pointe Levy

No.	Name	Age	Date	Father	Mother	Townland	Parish	County	Ship	Notes
577	CAUL, Margaret	14	07/48	?	?	?		?	?	Mrs. James Brooman
598	CLARK, Margaret	14	07/48	?	?	?		?	?	Télesphore Méthot, Ste. Croix
587	COLEMAN, Margaret	10	07/48	?	?	?		?	?	John Marshall, rue Collins
531	CONWAY, Catherine	9	06/22/48	?	?	?		?	John Bolton	Sent to Montreal (parents)
530	CONWAY, Mary	10	06/22/48	?	?	?		?	John Bolton	Sent to Montreal (parents)
539	CORCORAN, Ann	6	06/22/48	?	?	?		?	Lady Milton	Mr. Y. Murray (Stevedne), Diamond Harbour
466	COUGHLAN, Johanna	12	06/02/48	Owen	Biddy Nealan	Coalmeals		Clare	Governor	Dr. Têtu, Riv.-Ouelle
467	COUGHLAN, Joseph	7	06/02/48	Owen	Biddy Nealan	Coalmeals		Clare	Governor	Médard Boucher, Riv. Ouelle
593	DALY, Mary	14 months	07/48	?	?	?		?	?	Michel Falls, Petite Rivière
526	DENISON, Michael	4	06/22/48	?	?	?		?	Columbia	Mr. Charles
525	DENISON, Thomas	8	06/22/48	?	?	?		?	Columbia	Thomas Burns (Grocer), Diamond Harbour
509	DORSY, ?	14	06/19/48	?	?	?		?	?	Mr. Drolet
510	DORSY, ?	12	06/19/48	?	?	?		?	?	Mr. Drolet
586	FLYNN, Catherine	?	07/48	became a religious, Couvent Jésus Marie, Lévis						Jos Gingras, St. Antoine
52	FLYNN, Catherine	7	06/22/48	?	?	?		?	Scotland	Farmer in St. Nicolas
521	FLYNN, Honora	13	06/22/48	?	?	?		?	Scotland	Mr. Sheaver, Diamond Harbour
524	FLYNN, Jeremiah	3	06/22/48	?	?	?		?	Scotland	Marc Marceau
523	FLYNN, Thomas	5	06/22/48	?	?	?		?	Scotland	Henry Barry, Diamond Harbour
495	FRANKLIN, Johanna	16	08/04/48	John	Mary Ryan	Dool	Thorny Close	Limerick		Charles H. Têtu, Riv. Ouelle thence to N.Y
617	FITZPATRICK, Cath.	10	07/48	Went to sister, Mrs Trainer, St. Johnsbury Vermont		Kowes		Kilkenny	Progress	Dr. Rousseau, Nicolet
583	FITZPATRICK, Ellen	6	07/48	* Returned to her mother in 1848 to St. Johnsbury Vermont		Kowes		Kilkenny	Progress	Mrs. Doyer*, Faubourg St. Jean
616	FITZPATRICK, John	13	07/48	?	?	Kowes		Kilkenny	Progress	Dr. Rousseau, Nicolet
609	FITZPATRICK, Rich.	6	07/48	?	?	Kowes		Kilkenny	Progress	Michel Lemay, St. Grégoire
491	GOYHIMS, Honora	12	07/25/48	Austin	Honora Holland	Mockwaugh		Mayo	Congress	Left with brother on 07/31/48
584	GREEN, Bridget	?	07/48	?	?	?		?	?	Mrs. Joseph Gosselin
527	GRIFFIN, Michael	8	06/22/48	?	?	?		?	Clarendon	Mr. Pat Lambert, Près-de-ville

ÉTÉ 1848 / SUMMER OF 1848

No. Rég. Reg. No.	Nom Name	Âge Age	Date d'entrée Date of Entry	Père Father	Mère Mother	Paroisse Parish	Comté County	Bateau Vessel	Adopté par Adopted by
528	GRIFFIN, Patrick	6	06/22/48	? (died)	?	?	?	Clarendon	Mr. Laigeau Près-de-ville
529	GRIFFIN, Thomas	3 or 4	06/22/48	(died)	?	?	?	Clarendon	Mr. Bélanger Près-de-ville
578	HARRINGTON, Marg.	15	07/48	?	?	?	?	?	Mr. Basile Fortier St. Antoine
506	HETHRINGTON, George	9	06/10/48	?	?	?	?	?	Mr. Miles Kelly Diamond Harbour
573	HOPPER, John	13	07/48	?			?	?	Mr. O'Neil (Painter)
576	HOPPER, Julia	8	07/48	?			?	?	Faubourg St. Louis
575	HOPPER, ?	?	07/48	?			?	?	Mrs. Newhile Sault-en-Matelot
574	HOPPER, Helen	10	07/48	?	?	?	?	?	Joseph Bergeron
606	HORRIGAN, James	8	07/48	?	?	?	?	?	St. Grégoire
534	HUGHES, Margaret	7	06/22/48	?	?	?	?	Clarendon	Mr. McCarty Près-de-ville
464	HURLEY, Ann	13	06/02/48	John	Honora Finikan	Coalmeals	Clare	Governor	Pascal Dumais Kamouraska
465	HURLEY, Ellen	11	06/02/48	John	Honora Finikan	Coalmeals	Clare	Governor	Vital Harvey Malbaie
497	HURLEY, Jane	18	08/16/48	John	Honora Finikan	Coalmeals	Clare	Governor	Pascal Dumais Malbaie
545	JENNINGS, John	9	06/22/48	?	?	?	?	?	?
482	JOICE, Honora	18	06/27/48	John	Sealy Joice	Clifden	Galway	St. John	Dr. Poulin Rimouki
481	JOICE, Mary	16	06/27/48	John	Sealy Joice	Clifden	Galway	St. John	Mr. Henri Martin Rimouski
597	KANE, Catherine	9	07/48	?	?	?	?	?	Mrs. Canichon St. Roch
582	KAVANNAH, Lawrence	8	07/48	?	?	?	?	?	Antoine Maher St. Catherine
558	KEEGAN, Peter	10	06/29/48	?	?	?	?	Aberdeen	Mr. Pat Shee (dry goods) Basse Ville
559	KEEGAN, Rosa	8	06/29/48	?	?	?	?	Aberdeen	Mr. Pat Shea Basse Ville
599	KELBOY, Martin	11	07/48	?	?	?	?	?	Mr. F.X. Legendre St. Antoine
594	KENNEDY, Steven	4	07/48	?	?	?	?	?	Mr. Isaie Lemay Lotbinière

139

No.	Name	Age	Date	Father	Mother	Townland	County	Ship	Notes
544	KENNY, Bridget	7	06/22/48	?	?	?	?	?	Mr. Larivière / St. Roch
613	KELLY, Ann	5	07/48	?	?	?	?	?	Legendre Grenier / St. Grégoire
537	KELLY, Mary	1	06/25/48	?	?	?	?	Primrose	Mr. Fréchette
519	KILBOY, Catherine	6	06/22/48	?	?	?	?	Clarendon	Mr. Maher*
516	KILBOY, Honora	18	06/22/48	?	?	?	?	Clarendon	Entered service m.a Philips in Boston
518	KILBOY, John	8	06/22/48	?	?	?	?	Clarendon	Mr. Lafontaine / New Liverpool
517	KILBOY, Margaret	14	?	?	?	?	?	Clarendon	Entered service m.a Furlong in New Ireland / Mrs. Lynch (died)
543	KOONY, Pat	1	06/22/48	?	?	?	?	?	Returned to father in N.Y.
477	LALLY, Mary	5	06/20/48	John	Mary	Killadoon	Sligo	Dromahair	Mr. Donohue
571	LAVERY, ?	7	07/48	?	?	?	Was adopted at the age of twelve	?	Mr. Neville
570	LAVERY, William	7	07/48	?	?	?	Was adopted at the age of twelve	?	?
572	LAVERY, ?	10	07/48	?	?	?	Was adopted at the age of twelve	?	?
614	LAWLER, Catherine	8	07/48	?	?	?	?	?	Returned to father
615	LAWLER, Ellen	6	07/48	?	?	?	?	?	Returned to father
487	LYNCH, Mathew	14	06/30/48	?	?	Corte Hill	Cavan	Retriever	Sent to father in N.Y.
533	McCARRIGAN, Cath.	3	06/22/48	?	?	?	?	Dykes	Mr. Petit / Près de ville
535	McCONNELL, Charlotte	7	06/22/48	?	?	?	?	?	Mr. Gouin / Près de ville
507	McDONALD, Henry	5	06/19/48	?	?	New Caledon	Tyrone	Lady Gordon	Mr. Thomas Bogue (Grocer) / Diamond Harbour
508	McDONALD, John	10	06/19/48	?	?	New Caledon	Tyrone	Lady Gordon	Mr. Curtain
611	McGOURTY, Cecily	7	07/48	?	?	became a religious in St. Grégoire	?	?	Mr. J.B. Rouleau / St. Grégoire
612	McGOURTY, Margaret	7	07/48	went to Brooklyn	?	?	?	?	Mr. J.B. Bourbeau / St. Grégoire
496	McGUIRE, Jane	18	08/14/48	William	Jane Hays	Drumlin	Cavan	Jonah Elgin	A.C. de Lachevrotière / Lotbinière / (m. Gr. Commerford in Brooklyn N.Y.)
589	McINTYRE, Catherine	4	07/48	?	?	?	?	?	Died
596	McMAHON, Catherine	14	07/48	?	?	?	?	?	F.X. Fecteau / Lotbinière
556	McREAVY, Anne	8	06/25/48	?	?	?	?	Pursuit	Mr. Moriarty
555	McREAVY, Sarah	14	06/25/48	?	?	?	?	Pursuit	Mr. Kelly
494	MAHONY, Ann	3	08/01/48	?	?	?	?	?	Ant. Larouche / Rimouski
470	MAHONY, Bridget	12	06/02/48	Patrick	Honora Kelly	Coalmeals	Clare	Governor	Johnny Mavinon (?) / Rimouski

* Child was taken away from Mr. Maher & returned to her sister Mrs. Furlong.

ÉTÉ 1848 / SUMMER OF 1848

No. Rég. Reg. No.	Nom Name	Âge Age	Date d'entrée Date of Entry	Père Father	Mère Mother	Paroisse Parish	Comté County	Bateau Vessel	Adopté par Adopted by
471	MAHONY, Catherine	7f	06/02/48	Patrick	Honora Kelly	Coalmeals	Clare	Governor	Étienne Pineau Rimouski
566	MAHONY, Margaret	11	07/06/48	?	?	?	?	Agnes	Mr. Falconbridge Connituber
472	MAHONY, Mary	13	06/02/48	Patrick	Honora Kelly	Coalmeals	Clare	Governor	Ant. Larouche Rimouski
546	MEEKE, ?	1	06/22/48	?	?	?	?	?	Mrs. Bellavance Près de ville (died)
538	MILLIGAN, Catherine	6	06/22/48	?	?	?	?	Lady Milton	Ebz. Servant Près de ville
492	MOGAN, Catherine	9	07/29/48	?		?	?	St. John	Zephirin Pineau Rimouski
493	MOGAN, Mary	3	07/29/48	?		?	Galway	St. John	Jean B. Corriveau Rimouski
500	MONAGHAN, Thaddeus	8	06/10/48	?	?	?	?	Agnes	Denis McDevitt Champlain St.
480	MOYLICAN, ?	16	06/23/48	?	?	?	?	Governor	Joined service 07/01/48
565	MUBROG, Owen	7	06/29/48	?	?	?	?	Anne	Joseph Neville Tibbitt's Cove
469	MURPHY, Catherine	10	06/02/48	Michael	B. Handrahan	Coalmeals	Clare	Governor	Returned to father
468	MURPHY, Harriet	12	06/02/48	Michael	B. Handrahan	Coalmeals	Clare	Governor	Returned to father
484	NEALON, Edward	11	06/30/48	James	Honora Moylan	Coalmeals	Clare	Governor	Cornelius McCarthy St. Catherine
483	NEALON, James	15	06/30/48	James	Honora Moylan	Coalmeals	Clare	Governor	Dennis McCarthy St. Catherine
520	NOLAN, William	8	06/22/48	?	?	?	?	Wandsworth	Pat McMahon
562	O'BRIEN, John	6	06/29/48	?	?	?	?	?	Mr. Chrisman St. Roch
502	O'CONNELL, Ellen	12	06/10/48	?	?	?	?	Urania	Mr. Ed. Lachance Près de ville
505	O'CONNELL, Honora	3½	06/10/48	?	?	?	?	Urania	Mr. Fer. Bedard Près de ville
504	O'CONNELL, Margaret	6½	06/10/48	(died)	?	?	?	Urania	Miss Mary Curtain Près de ville
503	O'CONNELL, Mary	8½	06/10/48	(died)	?	?	?	Urania	Patrick Kennedy Près de ville
600	O'DONELL, Margaret	9 months	07/48	?	?	?	?	?	Mrs. Hudevin rue d'Aiquillon Qué.

ID	Name	Age	Date	Father	Mother	Townland	County	Ship	Remarks
554	O'GRADY, Alicia	1	06/25/48	(died)	?	?	?	Jessie	Mrs. Godie / Later claimed
552	O'GRADY, Bridget	8	06/25/48	?	?	?	?	Jessie	by uncle in Bytown / Denis Maguire
553	O'GRADY, Patrick	7	06/25/48	?	?	?	?	Jessie	Later clamed by uncle / Mr. Fox / Beauport
541	O'LEVY, Johanne	7	06/22/48	?	?	?	?	Scotland	Mr. Copn. O'Leary / Diamond Harbour
542	O'LEVY, John	3	06/22/48	?	?	?	?	Scotland	Mr. Bedard / Diamond Harbour
585	O'MILAY, Ann	9	07/48	?	?	?	?	?	Patrick Fitzsimmons / Quebec
532	PATES, Bridget	12	06/22/48	?	?	?	?	?	Sent to Montréal to Parents
619	PATRYVANNY, Marg.	9	07/48	?	?	Bann	Mayo	Columbia	Étienne Nourriet (Parmenties) / Nicolet
618	PATRYVANNY, Patrick	11	07/48	?	?	Bann	Mayo	Columbia	Étienne Nourriet / Nicolet
551	REGAN, Catherine	2	06/24/48	?	?	?	?	Lotus	Mr. Gignac / Près de ville
550	REGAN, John	5	06/24/48	?	?	?	?	Lotus	Denis Cantillon (culler) / Quebec
511	RIGNEY, Catherine	18	06/22/48	?	?	?	?	Clarendon	In service
512	RIGNEY, Margaret	14	06/22/48	?	?	?	?	Clarendon	In service
515	RIGNEY, Michael	5	?	?	?	?	?	Clarendon	Cap Rouge
513	RIGNEY, Pat	15	06/22/48	?	?	?	?	Clarendon	Thomas Bogue (Grocer) / Diamond Harbour
514	RIGNEY, William	10	06/22/48	?	?	?	?	Clarendon	Mr. Airly / Cap Rouge
581	RYAN, Honora	3	07/48	James	Catherine Brennan	Monnan	Kilkenny	Coromandel	Antoine Petit / St. Roch
579	RYAN, Lawrence	12	07/48	James	Catherine Brennan	Monnan	Kilkenny	Coromandel	George Tremblay / Percé
580	RYAN, Michael	10	07/48	James	Catherine Brennan	Monnan	Kilkenny	Coromandel	Dr. Hannick / Percé
548	RULAN, Judith	1	06/22/48	?	?	?	?	?	Mrs. Marcoux / Près de ville
488	SCANLON, Nancy	6	06/30/48	John	Mary Wynn	Riverstown	Sligo	Dromahair	Sent to father in Guelph 07/12/48
489	SCANLON, William	5	07/10/48	John	Mary Wynn	Riverstown	Sligo	Dromahair	Sent to father in Guelph 07/12/48
462	SHALLOO, Catherine	5	06/02/48	Patrick	Ellen Handrahan	Coalmeals	Clare	Governor	Antoine Girard / Pte Levy

ÉTÉ 1848 / SUMMER OF 1848

No. Rég. Reg. No.	Nom Name	Âge Age	Date d'entrée Date of Entry	Père Father	Mère Mother	Paroisse Parish	Comté County	Bateau Vessel	Adopté par Adopted by
463	SHALLOO, John	4	06/02/48	Patrick	Ellen Handrahan	Coalmeals	Clare	Governor	Died June 4
479	SHALLOO, Patrick	6	06/23/48	Patrick	Ellen Handrahan	Coalmeals	Clare	Governor	Narcisse Banville Rimouski
478	SHALLOO, Thomas	13	06/23/48	Patrick	Ellen Handrahan	Coalmeals	Clare	Governor	Major Joseph Samson Pointe Lévis
610	SHEHAN, Catherine	9	07/48	?	?	?	?	?	Antoine Bédard Trois-Rivières
595	SHINE, Ellen	?	07/48	?	?	?	?	?	Her sister
601	SHRAHAN, John	4	07/48	?	?	?	?	?	Mrs. Pierre Petit St. Roch
461	SLATTERY, Ann	14	07/02/48	Darby	Mary Dunlan	Liverpool		?	Mr. Drouin St. Antoine
602	SULLIVAN, Bridget	13	07/48	?	?	?	?	?	J.B. Boudreau St. Grégoire
561	TIERNY, Margaret	6	06/29/48	?	?	?	?	Jane Grey	James Byrne (Timber tower) Champlain St.
590	TYRELL, Edward	11	07/48	?	?	?	?	?	Michael McCollough St. George
607	TYRELL, Patrick	13	07/48	?	?	?	?	?	Antoine Desauniers St. Grégoire (to N.Y.)
608	TYRELL, Thomas	7	07/48	?	?	?	?	?	Moïse Laplante St. Grégoire
604	WALSH, Anne	8	07/48	?	?	?	?	?	Pierre Poirier St. Grégoire
603	WALSH, Margaret	10	07/48	M. Thomas Davy of 1847 list			?	?	Joseph Prince St. Grégoire
605	WALSH, Robert	7	07/48	became a priest		?	?	?	Joseph Pavre St. Grégoire
563	WARD, Julia	10	06/29/48	?	?	?	?	Rose	James Neville Tibbit's Cove

143

APP. 2

LETTERS FROM GROSSE ILE

LETTRES DES PRÊTRES DE GROSSE-ÎLE

TRANSLATION

Grosse Ile June 13, 1847

My Lord, (Joseph Signay, Bishop of Quebec)

I received yesterday the letter that your Grace kindly addressed to me. The work here, though it was diminished, suffices to keep us constantly occupied. The number of sick rises to between 13 and 1400. On Friday there were 67 deaths, and the day before an even greater number.

Mr. McDonald and Mr. Trahan are full of courage and good will but I believe that a rest would be good for both of them, especially for Mr. Trahan who was complaining yesterday of lassitude, and this morning about a headache. Mr. McDonald has a bad cold, but apart from that is pretty well.

A new hospital has just been finished with 122 beds, the sick will be placed there today or tomorrow. Two other similar buildings are being constructed. The arrival of more ships with many sick on board has also been announced to us.

The care of the sick is better now than it was. There are a number of cooks and nurses, but never enough. From every side people are asking for food, and when you see how thin most of these poor wretches are, you have no doubt that lack of food is the principal cause of all their sickness.

> *Respectfully*
> *My Lord*
> *Your Grace's most humble and*
> *obedient servant*
> *E.J. Horan, priest.*

> Source: Archives Diocèse Ste Anne de
> la Pocatière.

ORIGINAL

Une heure (no date)

Monseigneur, (Joseph Signay, Évêque de Québec)

Nous sommes arrivés après le plus heureux voyage. Il y a environs quarante batiments (sic) dans le port dont une douzaine ou plus ont été visités. Dans les hôpitaux il y a, selon M. Symes, douze cents malades dont moins de la moitié attendent les derniers secours. La plupart meurent aussitôt qu'ils ont été administrés et sont remplacés par d'autres. On ne croit pas qu'il en soit encore mort sans sacrement. Hier, il y a eu environ 55 enterrements en tout. M. McGuirk est assez bien, M. McGauran un peu moins et M. McDevitt est bien faible. Il y a trois conversions. Le nombre total des émigrés est estimé à dix mille. Il y a des malades à bord de tous les batiments, plus ou moins, en tout environs mille. Demain, l'Église sera occupée, il y a trente six tentes remplies. D'après un coup d'œil jeté en passant dans les hôpitaux, nous avons des scènes déchirantes. M. McGauran, M. McDevitt et M. McGuirk seraient trop faibles pour résister longtemps. Ils pensent que six missionnaires vigoureux feront l'affaire, si une fois ils peuvent reprendre le dessus sur le surcroît continuel d'ouvrage. Je n'ai pu les voir qu'un instant parce qu'on est venu les chercher en grande hâte. Nous allons partir à l'instant pour les hopitaux où on nous promet de la besogne. M. McGauran ne peut pas entendre parler de monter à Québec. J'oserai demander à votre grandeur de faire l'impossible pour envoyer trois nouveaux prêtres au moins pour quelque jours jusqu'à ce qu'on ait fait face au plus pressé et pris le dessus.

Excusez, Monseigneur, cette lettre écrite à la hâte et sans suite. Je n'ai vu les missionnaires qu'une minute parce qu'on les demandaient. Ils me chargent de vous offrir leurs respects.

Daignez aussi, Monseigneur, me recommander au Seigneur et le prier de nous donner des forces.

E.A. Taschereau, ptre.

Source: Archives Diocèse Ste Anne de la Pocatière.

TRANSLATION of above

One o'clock (no date)

My Lord,

We arrived after a very lucky trip. There are about forty ships in the port of which a dozen or more have been visited. According to Mr. Symes there are about 1200 sick about half of whom await the last rites. Most of them die as soon as they have received the sacraments, and are replaced by others. We don't believe that any die without the sacraments. Yesterday there were about 55 burials in all. Mr. McGuirk is pretty well, Mr. McGauran less so, and Mr. McDevitt very weak. There have been three conversions. The total number of immigrants is estimated at ten thousand. There are sick people aboard every ship, probably about a thousand. Tomorrow the church will be filled; thirty-six tents are already filled. Even a glance into any of the hospitals reveals heart-rending scenes. Mr. McGauran, Mr. McDevitt and Mr. McGuirk will be too weak to resist the disease much longer. They think that six strong missionaries would do, if once we could get ahead of the continual overlapping of work. I did not see them for very long because they were summoned in great haste. We are about to leave for the hospitals where we have been assured of lots of work. Mr McGauran will not hear of going up to Quebec. I dare ask Your Grace to do the impossible and send three more priests at least for a few days until we have looked after those in the greatest need, and gotten ahead of the work.

Please excuse this letter written in haste and disconnected. Because they were in demand, I saw the missionaries for only a minute.

They asked me to offer you their respects.

I ask you, My Lord to pray for me, and to ask the Lord for strength for us.

E.A. Taschereau, priest.

(Robert Symes, commissary officer, secular volunteer)
(James McDevitt, Hugh McGuirk, priests)

TRANSLATION

May 30, 1847

My Lord,

The Saint George has just anchored near the ship where I have been hearing confessions for four hours. Hearing it arrive, I hasten to acknowledge reception of your last two letters. I assure you, My Lord, that those letters were very consoling, coming as they do from a heart that is full of a father's tenderness. Mr. McDevitt's arrival made me very happy, and I put him to work immediately.

As for myself, My Lord, I have recovered from my fatigue, not because I have rested but because I have become accustomed to it. I don't feel it any more. I assure you, My Lord, that I have never in my life felt such consolation, the blessings of the sick and the dying sweeten all our pains. You have announced that you are sending Mr. McDonnell to me; again, My lord, a sign of the care that you have for the mission that I lead. But I think we could let things go on like this for a while, I believe that we can manage, the three of us at present, to handle all the work and I can very well say that I would like to force myself a little bit more, and my zealous fellow workers feel the same, that to have someone else come, who, experience has taught us would want things his way. With all possible submission, My Lord, I prefer not to have anyone else at present. We have no place to put anyone, our little castle is already filled.

There are increasing deaths on board the ships. Today we buried nearly fifty from off the ships. I hope that things will be better.

Please excuse the condition of this letter. I am writing on shipboard, I do not have the time to go to the house, the steamboat is ready to leave.

I am your Grace's most devoted servant,

B. McGauran, priest

ORIGINAL

Monseigneur,

À mon arrivée ici j'ai trouvé l'état de la Grosse Île (sic) bien amélioré. Ce n'est plus la Grosse Île de mon temps (sic) cependant on y trouve encore des cas de la plus triste nature. Il est bon que je vous dise à votre grandeur que je me porte très bien, je puis ajouter aussi que je suis très content. Il en est de même des braves Mr. Ferland et McDonnell.

Je voudrais, Monseigneur, attirer votre attention sur la question d'avoir un cheval au service des Missionnaires ici, qu'il soit acheté ou loué pour la saison. Il est vrai que Dr. Douglas nous prête, comme il dit, sa voiture pour aller au Camp de Santé, (the tents for the waiting healthy passengers) une fois par jour, mais lorsqu'il arrive que nous y sommes appelés la nuit ou que le dit docteur manque à sa promesse, nous sommes obligés de faire une demie lieu à pied, chose désagréable pour des personnes qui viennent de passer deux ou trois heures debout à parcourir les hopitaux. Je laisse, Monseigneur, la chose à votre considération.

Je suis de votre Grandeur le très humble et dévoué serviteur.

B. McGauran, ptre.

TRANSLATION OF ABOVE

September 2, 1847

My Lord,

On my arrival here I found that the condition of Grosse Ile is much better. It is not the Grosse Ile of my time, but one can still find some very sad cases. I must tell you that I am very well, and I am very happy. It is the same for the brave Mr Ferland and Mr McDonnell.

I would, my Lord, like to draw your attention to our need for a horse to be of service here, either bought or rented for the season. It is true that Dr. Douglas lends us his horse & cart once a day to go to the tents where the healthy passengers wait, but when we're called in the middle of the night, or the doctor forgets his promise, we are obliged to go a mile and a half on foot, and that is pretty demanding on people who have just spent two or three hours on their feet in the hospitals. I leave the matter to your consideration.

I am, Your Grace's most humble and devoted servant,

B. McGauran

(Jean-Baptiste-Antoine Ferland, priest
J. McDonnell, priest)

APP. 3

REPORT OF VESSELS BOARDED AT THE QUARANTINE STATION
JULY 1847 (EXCERPT)

RAPPORT DES VAISSEAUX VISITÉS À LA QUARANTAINE
JUILLET 1847 (EXTRAIT)

REPORT of Vessels Boarded at the Quarantine Station, Grosse Isle:

From 11th July 1847 — To 17th July, 1847

RIG—and NAME.	CAPTAIN'S NAME.	From,	Date of Sailing,	Arrival,	At what hour boarded,	Cargo,	Passengers. Cabin.	Steerage.	Consigned to,	No. of Days Quarantine	Date of release,	H. H.	Si. Si.	REMARKS.
211 Brig Gilson Griend	Hugh Poole	London	May 27th	July 11th	11t	Ballast	167	449	Master		July 12			
212 Ship Charlotte	Rich'd Brewery	Plymouth	June 2nd	"	11t	Ballast	6	332	J. C. Lee		12	2		
213 Bark Ceylon	John Crystal	New York	" 16th	"	11t	Ballast			Order		14	2	1	
214 Bark Albert	James Laughlan	Waterford	" 5	"	11t	Ballast		234	Caryan & Co		15	9	4	
215 Brig John Jardine	James Gunton	Liverpool	" 11	"	11t	Ballast		354	Benson		15/13	8		
216 Ship Manchester	Peter Burne	Liverpool	" 5	"	11t	Ballast		313	Caryan & Co		21	9	11	
217 Ship Jessie	William Oliver	Cork	" 8	"	11t	Ballast	4	457	J. Wilson		12 55	44		
218 Brig Perseverance	Henry Briggs	Hamburgh	May 18th	"	11t	General		165	Pigeon Pickles & Co		12	4		
219 Ship Kind Queen	John David	Newport	June 1st	"	11t	Ballast	1	577	Orier		19 130	65		
220 Bark Sarah	George Fletcher	Liverpool	July 29	"	12t	General	6	241	Orier		12 31	31		
221 Bark Floyd	Wm Rathburn	Sligo	" 1st	"	12t	General	8	204	Liverpool & Co		13	2		
222 Bark Reg & Adelaide	Ariel Smith	Waterford	" 29	"	13t	Ballast		198	Orier		13			
223 Bark Rosena	William McShain	Cork	June 24	"	12t	Ballast	2	354	Orier		15 19	3		
224 Bark Princess	Dan Murphy	Bremen	May 24	"	12t	Ballast	2	318	J. McLean		12 1	1		
225 Ship Triton	James Smith	Liverpool	" 18	"	12t	Ballast	10	463	Raven & Co		32 103	93		
226 Ship Thistle	James Jarmer	Liverpool	June 1st	"	12t	Ballast		382	J. C. Lee		15 13	2		
227 Ship Avon	Fred Johnston	Cork	May 19	"	13t	Ballast	3	350	J. White		26 140	134		
228 Brig Wonder	Thos Hunter	Sligo	June 3	"	13t	Iron	3	176	Master		14 1	2		
229 Brig Pallas	Abbot Reid	Bremen	May 19	"	14t	Ballast		153	Victor Vancel		14 1	2		
230 Schr Emmaline	S. B. Hubant	Pictilouche	June 29	"	14t	Ballast		15	Master		14			
231 Brig Nancy	William Epton	Sligo	May 24	" 17	17t	Ballast		154	J. C. Lee		25	5	2	
							210				Total			

REPORT of Vessels Boarded at the Quarantine Station, Grosse Isle:

No 13

From 27th July 1847 &c &c &c to 31st July 1847

No.	RIG and NAME.	CAPTAIN'S NAME.	From,	Date of Sailing,	Arrival,	At what hour boarded.	Cargo,	Passengers. Cabin,	Passengers. Steerage.	Consigned to,	No. of Days Quarantine,	Date of release.	REMARKS.
253	Bark Jamestown	R. James	Newport	June 1st	July 27		Ballast	22.0	189	H.L. Brientfall		July 28	1
254	Brig Argo	P. Season	Sligo	" 11	" 27		Ballast	"	127	Order		" 30	2 3
255	Schr Heroine	D. Walker	Aberdeen	May 29	" 27		Ballast	6	74	Leverrier		" 28	
256	Bark Sir H. Pottinger	R. Cowel	Cork	" 29	" 28		Ballast	1	399	A.B. Brientfall		Aug 3	106
257	Bark George	W. Sheridan	Dublin	" 28	" 28		Ballast		104	Order		" 1	2 6
258	Brig Delta	R. Rutter	Bremen	" 24	" 28		Ballast		143	A. Joss & Co		July 28	3
259	Bark Ann Hill	W. Long	Sligo	" 23	" 28		Ballast	2	414	Order		" 2	11 12
260	Bark Broom	D. White	Liverpool	June 13	" 28		Ballast		515	Gilmour		" 5	62 16
261	Ship Blenheim	Alex Thomson	Baltimore & Cork	" 29	" 28		Ballast	6	398	Joss Agent		" 19	6 12
262	Bark Panteira	Will White	Limerick	" 11	" 28		Ballast		389	Rowan & Waterous		Aug 2	59 15
263	Ship Wingreard	Thos Austin	Liverpool	June 28	" 29		Ballast	1	1176	J. Beine		" 11	106 53
264	Brig Cumberland	J. M. Laird	Bremen	" 8	" 29		Ballast		365	Master		July 29	1
265	Brig Millwon	R. Lang	London	" 6	" 29		Ballast	7	215	Order		" 30	1
266	Brig York Shire	G. Judge	Leith	" 3	" 29		Ballast	4	292	Leverrier		Aug 10	40 45
267	Brig Lucy Lindsell	Thos Irvine	Cuxhaven	" 3	" 29		Ballast	1	241	Elmore		" 5	50 16
268	Bark Diamond	Wele Owen	Bremen	" 8	" 29		Ballast		166	Owen		July 30	2 5
269	Brig X L	John Arundel	Galway	" 11	" 30		Ballast	1	161	S. Wilson		" 30	3 2
270	Ship Cygnet	Geo Browne	New Orleans	" 1	" 30		Ballast	2	208	Gilmour		" 31	
271	Brig Martingale	Geo Browne	Hamburg	May 25	" 30		Ballast		168	Pegan & Holme		" 31	
272	Bark Basine	Thos Wilson	Northport	June 15	" 31		Ballast		334	Peele & Co		Aug 16	100 100

(handwritten signatures at bottom)

Table No 2

Nominal List of Persons who died in the Grosse Isle Hospital since First of May shewing in what manner the property was disposed of &c &c.

No	Names	Age	From what Vessel	From what Port	Date of Admission	Date of Death	Disease	Property how disposed of
1	Mrs Jane Begley	38	Bell Ann	Derry		18th Aug.t 1847	Typhus F.	Taken by the Friends
2	Bridget Phelan	21	"	Dublin		19th "	Typhus F.	Do
3	Ed. Flannigan	39	Mary	Cork		20th "	"	Do
4	Isabella Bibbens	1	Brig Wm Tell	Newry		20th "	Variola	Do
5	Eliza Bushell	6	Bell Mary	Cork		21st "	Diarrhea	Do
6	Mary Bushell	4 mo	"			21st "	Typhus Fev.	Do
7	Cath. Hitchcock	32	" Britton			22 d	Typhus F.	Do
8	Mary Ryan	4	Penny	Youghall		24th "	"	Do
9	John Ryan	3	" Mark	Cork		"	Diarrhea	Do
10	David Reilly	22	Ships Riddle	Limerick		30th "	Typhus Fev.	Do
11	David Walker	1 1/2	Bell Mary	Cork		26 -	Typhus F.	Do
12	Bridget Tenny	1	Penelope	Youghall		27th "	Typhus F.	Do
13	Anne Fitzpatrick	31	" Britton	Cork		20th "	"	Do
14	Eliza Butler	30	" Penelope			28th "	"	Do
15	Mary Kenny	19	"			32 d	"	Do
16	Ellen Leech	20	"			22 d	"	Do
17	John Wigmartin	6	"			31st "	Phthisck	Do
18	Cath. Maddem	2	Mary			29th "	"	Do
19	John Mustford	2	"			26th "	"	Do
20	Dorothy Dougherty	2	"			21st "	"	Do
21	Marg.t Grovel	3	" Britton			21st "	"	Do
22	Cath. Lawrlor	10	Mary			31st "	Diarrhea	Do
23	Ellen Lunston	8	"			29th "	Phthisck	Do
24	Wm Hurtnell	2	"			32 d	Diarrhea	Do
25	Michael Neil	34	"			4th "	Diarrhea	Do
26	Pat.t Lynch	36	Penny	Youghall		29th "	Typhus M.	Do
27	Ellen French	2	"	Cork		25th May	Phthisck	Do
28	John Philpson	26	Mary			29th "	Diarrhea	Do
29	Daniel Coughlan	1	"			29th "	Typhus M. Debilites	Do

155

No.	Names	Age	From what Vessel	From what Port	Date of Admission	Date of Death	Disease	Property how disposed of
30	Michael Doherty	6	Bark Mary	Cork	31st May	9th June	Marbut	Taken by the Friends
31	Michael Conolan	31	"	"	4th June	10th	Typhus F.	do
32	Michael Carmen	9mo	"	Limerick Cork	21st May	11th	Diarrhoea	do
33	Daniel McCarthy	34	Constantia	Cork	9th June	"	Feb. C.C.	do
34	Wm Murphy	32	Bark Mary	"	2	13th	Typhus F.	do
35	John Doherty	30	"	Dublin Cork	10th	14th	" F.	do
36	Bridget Dempsey	30	New Prospect	"	1st	16th	" C.C.	Sent to Quebec care of P. Murrin
37	Wm Leyzell	65	Bark Mary	"	3	17th	"	Taken by the Friends
38	Bridget Cazal	4	"	"	31st May	"	Feb. C.C.	do
39	Richard Cazal	6	"	"	"	"	Rubeola	do
40	Mary Cozal	6	"	"	3rd	19th	"	do
41	Bridget Bryan	22	Constantia	Limerick	9th	20th	Feb. C.C.	do
42	Wm Leyzell	65	Bark Mary	Cork	10th June	21st	Typhus F.	do
43	Mary Flyott	3	Constantia	Limerick	16th	20th	Feb. C.C.	do
44	Henry Lane	18	Bark Mary	Cork	15th May	22nd	Typhus F.	Sent to Quebec care of P. Murrin
45	John Beard	28	Triton N.	Dublin	8th June	23rd	"	Taken by the Friends do
46	John Lynch	23	Bark Mary	Cork	22nd May	26th	Typhus F.	£3.0.0 Paid to P. Murrin
47	Wm Leib	2	"	"	31st May	26th	Rubeola	Taken by the Friends
48	Patrick Wade	30	Maria	Quebec	8th June	28th	Typhus F.	do
49	Thos. Mursfoty	3	Ballymena	Cork	25th	28th	Feb. C.C.	Taken by the Friends
50	Thos. Fennel	18	Bark Mary	"	22nd May	30th	Typhus F.	do
51	Ellen Murrgott	10	Pendigot	Coghall Cork	26th May	6th July	Diarrhoea	Sent to Quebec care of P. Murrin
52	William John	6mo	Bark Mary	Dublin	11th June	6th	Typhus F.	Taken by the Friends
53	Margt Beard	32	Wm and Ann	Belfast	8th July	7th	Palsatinea	Sent to Quebec care of P. Murrin
54	Margt Harney	2	Marchborry	Cork	21st May	8th	Typhus F.	Sent to Quebec care of P. Murrin
55	Patm Harney	30	Bark Mary	Dublin	21st May	14th	"	1st June Sent to Quebec care of P. Murrin
56	James Goodson	29	New Prospect	"	8th June	16th	"	1st Sent to Quebec Sept 16th
57	Edwd Wagram	20	"	Cork	12th July	19th	"	Given to Fort Friends
58	James Mursfoty	13	Ursula	Ships	5th	"	Feb. C.C.	Sent to Quebec care of P. Murrin
59	Wm McHensh	10	Weser	Cork	12th	20th	Typhus F.	Portneright
60	Timothy Buckley	40	Ursula	"	19th	21st	Cholera	Given to the Colonie Bridgehart
61	Jacob Beard	20	Bark Mary	"	20th	22nd	Typhus F.	Taken by the Friends
62	Henry Langston	16	Servant in Ship	"	9th	"	"	

No.	Names	Age	Whom attended Visit	Whom attended Port	Date of Admission	Date of Death	Disease	Property how disposed of
63	Cath.e Sullivan	26	Ocilia	Cork	23d July	23d July	Cholera	Taken by his Friends
64	Daniel Leary	17	W.m Hartman	Belfast	23 "	23 "	"	do
65	James Collins	66	"	"	27 "	24 "	Fif.t brush/Cholera	do
66	Mary White	20	Ocilia	Cork	24 "	"	"	do
67	Bridget Dunn..	17	"	"	"	"	"	do
68	John Ryan	20	"	"	"	"	"	do
69	Marg.t Hogan	46	W.m Hartman	Belfast	25 "	25 "	Diarrhea Cholera	do
70	Hora Nagle	1	Ocilia	Cork	25 "	26 "	"	do
71	James Nunn	1	"	"	25 "	26 "	"	do
72	Margaret Nunn	50	"	"	26 "	"	"	do
73	John Twohig	11	"	"	"	24 "	"	do
74	Michael Murphy	56	"	"	27 "	"	"	do
75	Johannah Murray	29	"	"	24 "	"	"	do
76	Jerry Ryan	40	"	"	27 "	"	"	do
77	Darby Daly	20	"	"	28 "	28 "	"	do
78	Daniel Carroll	11	"	"	27 "	"	"	do
79	Johannah Solan	6	"	"	26 "	"	"	do
80	Esther Hallet	7	"	"	28 "	"	"	do
81	Paul Crowley	35	"	"	28 "	"	"	do
82	John Ryan	30	"	"	26 "	"	"	do
83	Jeremiah Buckley	23	"	"	26 "	29 "	"	Sent to Quebec care of D. Morrin
84	John Mc Carthy	26	"	"	28 "	"	"	Taken by his Friends
85	Timothy Bradley	5	Hosp.l Dep.t	Belfast	24 "	"	"	do
86	Cath. Driscoll	50	W.m Hartman	Cork	29 "	30 "	Feb. C.C.	do
87	Marg.t Barter	2	Ocilia	Belfast	24 "	"	Diarrhea Cholera	do
88	Riley Twohig	4	"	"	26 "	"	"	do
89	Mary Mc Donough	1½	W.m Hartman	"	29 "	30 "	"	do
90	Ellen Crowlet	7	Ocilia	Sligo	30 "	"	"	do
91	Paul Carroll	24	"	Chels	28 "	31 "	Typhus to Cholera	do
92	Edw.d Mc Culley	26	Belting Castle	Ocilia	30 "	"	"	do
93	Elizabeth Corman	18	"	"	"	"	"	do
94	Bryan Mc Inlis	3	Ocilia	"	"	"	"	do
95	James Tobin							do

157

No.	Names	Age	From what Vessel	From what Port	Date of Admission	Date of Death	Disease	Property how disposed of
96	James Court	2	Leila	Cork	28th July	31st July	Cholera	Taken by the Friends
97	Daniel Bryan	40	"	"	28 "	"	"	Do
98	Cath. Bryan	8	"	"	28 "	"	"	Do
99	... Newberry	24	New Prospect	Dublin	23 June	"	Typhus Fev.	Sent to Quebec care of Gt. Nivern
100	John Bryan	6	Leila	Cork	20 July	"	Cholera	Taken by the Friends
101	Walter Whitby	50	Amel Charlton	Dublin	20 July	"	"	Do
102	John Stephenson	28	Leila	Cork	23 "	"	"	Do
103	Mary Carbet	30	"	Belfast	24 "	"	"	Do
104	Robt. Corbet	34	Wm Heatman	Dublin	26 "	1st Augt	Fest. C.C. Cholera	Do
105	Margret McNann	5	Amel Charlton	Cork	26 Augt	"	Cholera	Do
106	James Conroy	28	Confience	Lisle	27 July	"	"	Do
107	John Nicholl	36	Wm Gittin	Londonderry	26 "	"	Typhus Fev.	Do
108	Jane Poster	3	Wm Heatman	Belfast	30 "	"	"	Do
109	Jane Monroe	22	Leila	Cork	1st Augt	3	Typhus Fev. M.	Given to her Brother
110	John Polder	4	"	"	29 July	"	Cholera	Taken by the Friends
111	Dorah Russell	14	Wm Heatman	"	19 "	"	"	Do
112	Wm Dodd	21	William	Lisburn	31 "	"	"	Do
113	Wm Beal	40	Thos. Gittin	Londonderry	30 "	3	"	Do
114	Bridget Pepont	11	Wm Heatman	Belfast	1st Augt	"	Hydroncephalus	Do
115	Hugh McLaughlan	3	Leila	Cork	1st "	"	Cholera	Do
116	Hugh Martin	60	Wm Heatman	Belfast	3 "	3	Diarrhoea	Do
117	Mary Bryan	2	Belay Castle	Sligo	3 "	"	Cholera	Do
118	Bridget Kelly	2	Wm Heatman	Belfast	3 "	4 "	"	Do
119	Ellen Graham	23	Leila	Cork	3 "	"	"	Sent to Quebec Care of Dr. Nivern
120	Josiah Jordan	19	Hanna	Limerick	3 "	"	"	Taken by the Friends
121	Ann McQueen	12	Wm Heatman	Belfast	20 "	"	Typhus M.	Do
122	Margt. McCabby	5	"	"	4 "	"	Cholera	Do
123	John Carr	5	"	"	3 "	"	"	Do
124	Wm O'Brien	2½	"	"	"	"	"	Do

No.	Names	Age	From what Vessel	From what Port	Date of Admission	Date of Death	Disease	Property how disposed of
129	Esqt Govan	2	Wm Heathman	Belfast	27th July	4th Augt	Cholera	Taken by the Friends
130	Philipt Betty	1	"	"	3d Augt	"	"	Do
131	Philip Ann Noble	18	"	"	4th	"	"	Do
132	Hellena Gullex	21	"	"	"	5th	"	Do
133	Esqt Slant	42	Oreka	Cork	"	"	"	Do
134	Mary Black	11	Wm Heathman	Belfast	"	"	"	Do
135	James Foyle	64	Capt Charlton	Dublin	3	"	"	Do
136	George McLogler	18	Wm Heathman	Belfast	4	"	"	Do
137	Philip Troubel	14	Chas Charlton	Dublin	5	"	"	Do
138	Wm Garret	38	Orela	Cork	"	"	"	Do
139	Crestian Conner	20			31st July	"	"	Do
140	John Water	5	Wm Heathman	Belfast	22d July	"	Typhus M	Do
141	John Beall	10	Belony Castle	Sligo	28th July	6	Cholera	Do
142	John Crosby	12	Chs Charlton	Dublin	20	"	Diarrhea	Do
143	John Leithly	16	Wm Heathman	Belfast	6th Augt	"	"	Do
144	Mary Beall	16	Belony Castle	Sligo	"	"	Typhus M	Do
145	James Hagan	25	Chs Charlton	Dublin	"	7th	Typhus M	Do
146	James Hamel	20	Wm Heathman	Belfast	3	"	Typhus G	Do
147	John Cushing	9	Best Mary	Cork	6	"	Cholera	Do
148	Aliya Wooll	6	Wm Heathman	Belfast	"	"	"	Do
149	Wm Cottenham	4	"	"	4th	"	"	Do
150	Sarah Worthly	54	Capt Charlton	Dublin	6th Augt	"	"	Do
151	Jams McCaugherty	20	Wm Heathman	Belfast	2	"	"	Do
152	Capt Stephent	27	"	"	7th	8th	"	Do
153	John Beall	9	Orela	Cork	8	"	"	Do
154	Ellen Donelb	14	"	"	3d	"	"	Do
155	Alex Low	3	Confeurence	Leith	31st July	"	"	Do
156	Roland Fitzher	24	Wm Heathman	Belfast	16th	"	"	Do
157	James Whiteman	21	"	"	6th	"	Typhus M	Do
158	Esqt Paul	50	Confeurence	Leith	7th	"	Cholera	Do
159	James Richie	14	Orela	Cork	6	9th	Diarrhea	Do
160	James Gatrold	6	Wm Heathman	Belfast	7	"	Cholera	Do
161	Margt Doyle	22	Chs Charlton	Dublin	9	"	Cholera	Do

No.	Names	Age	From what Vessel	From what Port	Date of Admission	Date of Death	Disease	Property how disposed of
162	Robt Horner	5	Chr Challin	Dublin	4 Augt	9 Augt	Cholera	Taken by the Friends
163	Crysfal Eastman	9	Bark Mary Mellon	Cork	9 "	"	"	do
164	Patk Vaugh	2	Mellon	Maryport	5 "	"	"	do
165	Patk Smith	—	Conference	Leith	4 "	"	"	do
166	John Mercer	62	Wm Redman	Belfast	9 "	"	"	Sent to Mr Buchanan Father for his Brother
167	Wilson Henry	—	Mellon	Maryport	9 "	"	"	Taken by the Friends
168	Wilson Hilton	11	Delia	Cork	9 "	"	"	do
169	Mary Ousley	11	Delia	Maryport	"	"	"	do
170	James Wright	60	Helyon	Maryport	"	"	"	do
171	Wm Fulton	20	Helyon	Wilton	9 "	10 "	"	do
172	Deborah McGovin	21	Eir Challin	Belfast	9 "	"	"	do
173	Robt Naugha	20	Wm Redman	Belfast	9 "	"	"	do
174	Michael Herman	1	Elgin	Belfast	"	"	"	do
175	John Healy	25	Chr Challin	Belfast	4 "	"	"	do
176	Jane Tansley	26	Wm Redman	Dublin	4 "	"	"	do
177	Mary McNamee	14	Chr Challin	Belfast	10 "	"	"	do
178	Robt Ferran	20	Wm Redman	Maryport	1 "	11 "	Typhus & Cholera	do
179	Ellen Scott	2	Donegal	Belfast	1 "	"	"	do
180	Robt Stuart	30	Wm Redman	Sligo	11 "	"	Typhus & Cholera	do
181	Patk Corner	12	Belay Castle	Sligo	"	"	"	do
182	Mary McFell	45	Conference	Maryport	"	12 "	"	do
183	Mary Dogolast	45	Donegal	Belfast	4 "	11 "	"	do
184	Saml McReilly	21	Chr Challin	Maryport	9 "	"	"	do
185	Robt Whiteman	27	Wm Redman	Belfast	"	"	"	do
186	Thos Scott	24	Donegal	Maryport	9 "	12 "	"	do
187	Mary Henry	25	Wm Redman	Belfast	9 "	"	"	do
188	Margt McFell	11	Conference	Leith	11 "	"	"	do
189	John Scott	60	Donegal	Maryport	12 "	13 "	"	do
190	Margt Serrold	6	Chr Challin	Wilton	8 "	"	"	do
191	John Serrold	4	"	"	10 "	"	"	do
192	John Gorman	4	"	"	13 "	"	"	do
193	Thos Quigley	30	Art Donegal	Sligo	4 "	"	"	do
194	Andrew White	80	Donegal	Molly Port	11 "	"	Typhus & Cholera	do

160

No.	Names	Age	From what Vessel	From what Port	Date of Admission	Date of Death	Disease	Property how disposed of
195	Patk Gorman	4	Chas Chaulten	Dublin	11th Augt	13th Augt	Cholera	Taken by the Friends
196	Joseph do	6	do	do	4th	14th "	"	do
197	Allen Carrington	6	Nelson	Maryport	13th	"	"	do
198	Susan McMurray	14	Chs Chaulten	Nelson	8th	"	"	do
199	Sally Grant	28	Nelson	do	12th	"	"	do
200	Eliza Grant	1	"	"	"	"	"	do
201	Ethel Carrington	4	Nelson	Maryport	13th	"	"	do
202	Elizth Hutchinson	33	Confiance	Sligo	11th	"	"	do
203	Ann Jordan	14	"	do	26th	16th	Typhus M & Cholera	do
204	Lucy Jordan	45	Cartwright	Nelson	14th	"	Cholera	do
205	Matk O'Brien	40	Talbotyn	Greenock	8th	"	Typhus M	do
206	Mary Brown	14	Stirling Castle	Belfast	14th	"	Typhus M	do
207	Patk Chaulten	40	Warren	Dublin	13th	"	Typhus G	do
208	Sarah Savage	40	Nelson	Belfast	26th July	"	Cholera	do
209	Thos Gorham	20	W. Huntman	Dublin	9th Augt	"	"	do
210	Thos Shane	9	Stirling Castle	Greenock	"	16th	"	Govt to decide case of St Kiern
211	John Hartnett	36	Stirling Castle	Cork	13th	"	Feb. C.C.	Taken by the Friends
212	Mary Mead	32	Odelia	Dublin	14th	"	Cholera	do
213	Wm Huntman	46	Nelson	Maryport	10th	"	Diarrhea	do
214	John Low	12	Confiance	Sligo	11th	"	Cholera	do
215	Geo. Kendrick	52	"	"	12th	"	"	do
216	James Graham	60	Nelson	Dublin	17th	"	Diarrhea	do
217	Wm Hutton	62	Chs Chaulten	"	9th	"	Cholera	do
218	Nichd McMurray	20	Stirling Castle	Greenock	16th	17th	"	do
219	Mary Palm	6	Lord	College	8th	"	"	do
220	Patrick Toby	54	Warren	Belfast	17th	"	"	do
221	Ann McAllister	41	Donegal	Maryport	14th	"	"	do
222	Daniel Hutchinson	8	do	"	7th	18th	"	do
223	Walter Best	2	Nelson	Dublin	18th	"	Veritt	do
224	Wm Clayborton	28	Nelson	"	13th	"	Diarrhea	do
225	Letitia More	24	"	"	18th	"	Cholera	do
226	Patk Martin	21	"	"	14th	"	"	do

No.	Names	Age	From what Vessel	From what Port	Date of Admission	Date of Death	Disease	Property how disposed of
224	Mary Barnes	36	Heber	Dublin	14th Augt	18th Augt	Cholera	Taken by the Friends
225	Isabella Grney	1	Girdelle	Liverpool	8th	19th	Diarrha	do
226	Betsey Grney	3	Donegal	Newport	13th	"	Diarrha	"
227	Catley Droldt	8	Wm Huelman	Belfast	8th	"	Cholera	Sent to Quebec care of Dr Moore
228	Robt Huelot	28	Donegal	Newport	19th	"		Taken by the Friends
229	Margt Lebiste	14	Nelson	Nelson	"	"		"
230	Stephen Salmon	2	Col Chatton		"	"		do
231	Eliza Barnes	24	Wm Huelman	Belfast	12th	20th		do
232	James Barnes	2	Nelson	Dublin	14th	"		do
233	Jno Teggar	60		Cork	8th	"		do
234	Jno Teggar	10	Ocilla	Newport	10th	"		do
235	Wm Mitchell	30	Donegal	Leith	6th	"		do
236	Thos Richard	10	Confuence			"		do
237	Thos Young	2		Dublin	16th	"		do
238	Owen Cunningham	10	Nelson		18th	23rd		do
239	*242 Edward McMahon	35		Dublin	18th	24th	Typhus R.	"
240	244 Alger McDougall	34	Stirling Cattle	Greenock	18th	24th	Cholera	Sent to Quebec care of Dr Moore
241	245 Mary Smith	1	Cwn Chatton	Dublin	8th	20th	"	Taken by the Friends
242	246 Danl McIver	26	Wm Huelman	Belfast	2nd	27th	"	do
243	246 Cath Belk	26	Col Chatton	Dublin	19th	27th	"	do
244	247 Wm Hegel	19	Nelson	Newport	22nd	27th		do
245	248 Conrad Ball	62	Donegal	"	20th	30th	Web C.C.	Sent to Quebec care of Dr Moore
246	249 Chester Degan	13	Heber	Dublin	24th	30th	Diarrha	Taken by the Friends
247	250 John Walter	3		Leith	30th	31st	Cholera	do
248	251 Margt Moffatt	49	Confuence	Belfast	12th	29 Sept	Feb C.C.	do
249	252 Ann Palmer	16	Wm Huelman	Dublin	24th	"		Vide John Perry
250	253 John Lindly	16	Col Chatton	Leith	25th	3	Cholera	Sent to Quebec care of Dr Moore
251	254 Andrew Mitchell	41	Confuence	Belfast	11th	5th	Web C.C.	Taken by the Friends
252	255 Jane McKaylags	50	Wm Huelman	Dublin	23rd	6th	Typhoid M	do
253	256 Bridget Huelt	36	Good	Newport	19th	"	Cholera	do
254	257 Gabriel Belk	28	Donegal	Leith	31st	6th	Diarrha	do
255	258 Robt Dalgleish	18	Confuence	"	11th	24th Augt	Cholera	Taken by the Friends
256	*243 Mary Wogg	32	"	"				

APP. 4

EXCERPTS FROM REGISTERS OF SAINT LUKE
OF GROSSE ILE

EXTRAITS DES REGISTRES DE SAINT-LUC
DE LA GROSSE-ILE

Le sujet du Mil huit cent quarante

Sept. Van Peter ... que avons ...

... devant le notaire ... lieu de ...

... de Patrick Pottery, âgé de cinq ...

... de Judith Darcy, âgée de ...

quarante ans, de John Barth, âgé ...

de quarante ans, et de quarante q ...

... autres ... devant les ...

... présents ... lieu ...

... dix-huit des années ... huit ...

Peter ... que ... dans ...

... les créatures du lieu ... trois ...

... devant le dit bâtiment ...

appelé Rose, ... autres des ... habitan ...

... présent John Baker, K. de ...

avec ... qui n'ont pas signé

Ald. M...

L'an mil huit cent quatre-vingt...

Marguerite
Elizabeth
Langlois.

L'an mil huit cent quatre-vingt...
sept, nous Prêtre soussigné avons baptisé
Marguerite Elizabeth, née le dix-sept du
présent mois, du mariage de Charles Langlois,
cultivateur, et de Hélène Chambers de
... St Luc, et la Sise ... Le parrain
a été Louis Langlois, soussigné, et la
Marraine Zoé Régina, qui n'a su
signer, le père absent.

Zoé Langlois
Laurent Fields
Marie Robinson

18.

166

TRANSLATION

Burial S8 (47 persons) — The 16th of June, eighteen forty seven, I the undersigned priest have buried in the cemetery of this place, the bodies of Patrick Slattery, aged five months, of Judith Darcy, aged five years, of John Booth, aged forty years, and of forty-four others unknown coming from different hospitals of the place.

Burial S9 (13 persons) — The eighteenth of the same month, I the undersigned priest have buried in the cemetery of this place, three persons unknown, from the Ship 'Rose', and ten others from the hospitals. Present John Noulin and Andrew Vincent who could not sign. E. de Montmagny, priest.

Baptism B4 The 20th June 1847. I the undersigned priest have baptized Marguerite Elizabeth, born the 18th of the lawful marriage of Charles Langlois, day labourer, and of Helen Chambers of St. Luke Island, called Grosse Ile. The godfather was Louis Langlois undersigned, and the godmother Zoé Vezina, who could not sign. Father absent.

P. Rose, priest

Signed: Louis Langlois
    Harriet Shields
    Amy Robinson

Burial S13 and following: This and the remainder are examples of the daily sad entries on the register of Saint Luc of Grosse Ile.

Le vingt-un juin, mil huit cent quarante-sept, nous
Prêtre soussigné, avons baptisé Ann, née depuis un
jour, du légitime mariage de Michael Hogue et
Jemmelie? & de Brigitt Duffy — Parrain Christophe
Lourion, marraine Ann Grace, qui, ainsi que le père
n'ont pas signé.

Le vingt deux juin, mil huit cent quarante sept, nous Prêtre soussigné, avons
inhumé dans le cimetière de l'Église
Luc côté le Gros ... le corps d'un nom-
...mé veuve Ann Avery, trente ... Grace,
Nostin et Andrew Brennent qui ...

(ne signer).

Th. M. Hé. Jean Pre

B.
Ann
Grace —

1 personne

168

APP. 5

SUMMARY OF BURIALS
REGISTER OF ST-LUKE
1847
TOTAL DES SÉPULTURES
SAINT-LUC DE LA GROSSE-ÎLE

1847

Nombre de sépultures faites chaque jour
durant la quarantaine dans qu'il ait été
possible de mentionner les nombres exacts

16	Juin	24 Trevans	36 no	25	Juillet	3e personne	43 r°
18	do	28	36 r°	26	do	15	44 r°
19	do	44	37 r°	27	do	31	44 r°
20	do	30	37 r°	28	do	1	44 r°
22	do	1	37 r°	29	do	38	44 r°
23	do	112	37 r°.38 r°	30	do	31	44 r°
24	do	44	38 r°	31	do	25	45 r°
25	do	37	38 r°	1	Août	27	45 r°
26	do	38	38 r°	2	do	31	45 r°
27	do	22	39 r°	3	do	13	45 r°
28	do	24	39 r°	4	do	20	45 r°
29	do	24	39 r°	5	do	24	47 r°

4 9bre	4 7bre	4 7bre	4 7bre	4 7bre	4 8bre	4 8bre	4 8bre	4 8bre	4 9bre	4 9bre	4 9bre	4 9bre	4 9bre	4 9bre	4 9bre	4 9bre
29	34	35	17	12	45	52	31	28	24	13	34	50	27	35	50	51
do	do	do	do	do	do	do	do	do	do	do	do	do	do	do	do	do
6	7	8	9	10	11	12	13	14	15	16	17	18	19	20	21	22
39bre	39bre	39bre	39bre	39bre	40bre	40bre	40bre	40bre	40bre	40bre	41bre	41bre	42bre	42bre	43bre	43bre
38	20	50	14	27	33	25	33	35	21	27	26	26	47	28	37	36
do	juillet	do	do	do	do	do	do	do	do	do	do	do	do	do	do	do
30	2	4	5	6	7	8	9	10	11	12	14	16	18	20	21	22

5Oro	40	de	23
5Tro	13 7bre	de	24
55Tro	14	7bre	22
55Tro	16	de	23
55roo	11	de	24
55roo	16	de	25
55roo	6	de	26
56ro	10	de	27
56ro	11	de	28
56ro	9	de	29
57roo	9	de	30
56roo	4	octobre	1
57Tro	9	de	2
57Tro	6	de	3
57rw	9	de	4
57rw	3	de	5
57rw		de	6

4Bro	29	de	23
4Boo	44	de	24
5Oro	34 primero	Aout	25
50ro	31	de	26
51ro	28	de	27
51roo	31	de	28
51Tro	24	de	29
51Tro	31	de	30
51ro	15	de	31
51roo	22	septembre	1
51roo	16	de	2
51ro	24	de	3
52ro	27	de	4
52ro	23	de	5
52roo	25	de	6
52oo	17	de	7
52oo	10	de	8

57ro	58ro	58ro	58ao	58no	58ro	59ro	59ro	59ro	59ro	59oo	59oo	59ao	60oo	60oo
8	8	7	6	3	4	3	4	4	2	2	2	4	3	
do	do	do	do	do	do	do	do	do	do	do	do	do	do	
7	8	9	10	11	12	13	14	15	16	17	18	19	20	

52oo	53ro	53ro	53ao	53oo	53oo	54ro	54ro	54ro	54oo	54oo	54oo	53ro
15	13	20	19	14	14	13	11	8	15	10	12	17
do	do	do	do	do	do	do	do	do	do	do	do	do
9	10	11	12	13	14	15	16	17	18	19	20	21

176

APP. 6

QUEBEC MERCURY
RETURN OF EFFECTS LEFT BY EMIGRANTS

LISTE DES EFFETS ET DE L'ARGENT LAISSÉS
PAR LES IMMIGRANTS

The Quebec  Mercury.

TUESDAY, NOVEMBER 2, 1847. MORES ET STUDIA ET POPULOS ET PRÆLIA DICAM. VIRG. GEO. IV.

VOLUME XLIII NUMBER 131.

RETURN of MONEY and EFFECTS left by EMIGRANTS, who died without relatives, at GROSSE ISLE, from the 16th May to 21st October, 1847.

Names.	Vessel in which Arrived.	Amount.			Remarks.
Catharine Mulholand,	Bark Syria,	1	5	5	William Barker Newton, Hamilton County, Armagh, Ireland.
Dennis Courtney,	Agnes,	0	4	6	
John Menechin,	Syria,	0	2	0	
John Boyle,	Ditto,	2	5	0	
Patrick O'Reilley,	Ditto,	2	1	1	
Thomas Newman,	Wandsworth,	0	1	0	
Nancy Rillie,	John Bolton,	0	19	0	
John Linn,	Bee,	0	2	6	
Andrew White,	Ditto,	0	5	0	
Jeremiah McCarty,	Ditto,	0	6	0	
Jeremiah Huggie,	Ditto,	0	1	6½	
William Dobbin,	Ditto,	1	0	0	
Patrick Carroll,	Wandsworth,	0	8	0	
Francis Mournie,	Bee,	0	1	0	
Mary Dean,	Syria,	0	3	0	
Mary McCachey,	John Bolton,	0	16	6	
James Small,	Ditto,	0	18	0	
Charles McKenzie,	Gilmour,	0	10	0	
John Garrely,	Dykes,	0	11	0	
Bridget Tabey,	Princess Royal,	10	2	6	
Mary Reynolds,	Ditto,	0	1	0	
Joseph Branegar,	Cape Breton,	0	1	6½	
Michael Fean,	Pursuit,	0	2	0½	
Anthony Hopkins,	Sisters,	9	15	0	
Alexander Brown,	Wilhelmina,	1	15	0	
Patrick Crowley,	Bee,	2	0	0	£1 Note Brother Jas, Ballanally, County Cork.
Ann McBrien,	George,	3	4	7	Jno. Ross, Aunagalgia, Cy. Fermanagh.

Names.	Vessel in which Arrived.	Amount.			Remarks.
Michael Flinn,	Yorkshire,	0	2	2½	
Bridget O'Meally,	Erin's Queen,	1	12	6	
James Tucker,	Larch,	0	18	0	Father Jas. Tucker, parish Arumcliffe, Sligo Post Office.
Bridget Wallace,	Virginia,	4	2	4	
George Gordon,	Saguenay,	0	9	0	
Bridget Corcoran,	Washington,	0	8	0	
Richard Dwyer,	Ditto,	0	10	6	
Judy Troy,	Odessa,	0	10	8½	
William Irvin,	John & Robert,	1	4	6	
Daniel Cline,	Naomi,	0	2	8	
Michael Conway,	Orderly,	0	12	0	
Edward Earl,	Steward Hamilton,	17	0	0	Brother Charles pepperds Castle parish Donougmore, County Wexford.
— Connagter,	Ditto,	0	4	10½	
Dennis Burns,	Covenanter,	0	2	6¼	
Ellen Courtain,	Saguenay,	0	12	6	
Sarah Hodgins,	Odessa,	0	7	0	
Catharine Casey,	Covenanter,	1	0	0	
Johnna. Laughlin,	Ditto,	0	8	6	
John Cassin,	Sobraon,	0	7	0	
Peter McDonough,	Larch,	0	2	4	
Anthony Manley,	Ganges,	1	0	9	
Johnna. Mead,	Ann Kenny,	0	8	8½	
Florius Sullivan,	Bridgeton,	1	12	6	
Catharine Rillie,	Superior,	3	7	7½	
Bridget Lawless,	Ditto,	0	14	5½	
Catharine Hunley,	Virginia,	0	3	7½	
Hugh Kennedy,	Bridgeton,	0	14	0	
Eliza Holden,	Coromandel,	1	0	0	

Name	Ship	£	s	d	Notes
Mary McCallister,	Superior,	0	9	0	
James Priest,	Wellington,	0	10	0	
Aron McFaddon,	Sir R. Peel,	0	5	0	
Isabella Tumbe,	Ditto,	0	13	8	
Edward Gilroy,	Argyle,	0	13	0	
Cathe. McGarachen,	Nurse from Quebec,	0	16	0	
Hugh Hetherington,	Dykes,	0	14	0	
Martin Highlands,	Emigrant,	0	6	0	
Michael Murphy,	Avon,	1	2	8	
James Dooley,	Washington,	0	4	8	
Cornelius Jeffy,	Free Trader,	0	18	0	
Bryan Ready,	Greenock,	1	7	0	
Mary Clark,	Champion,	100	0	0	8 Gold Rings.—Father, Jas. Pollard, Kilaba. parish Wicklif, care of Rev. Mr. Wright.
James English,	Coromandel,	1	8	6	Common Silver Watch.
Honora Gallacher,	Sir H. Pottinger,	1	10	1½	
James & Peter Hay,	Broom,	5	10	0	
Thomas Robinshall,	Yorkshire,				Seaman.
Samuel Long,	Rankin,	2	16	0	Ditto.
Alex. Sutherland,	Agnes,	2	2	0	Mate of the vessel.
Martin Bouch,	Aberdeen,	0	7	4	Ditto ditto.
Robert Stoba,	Lady Milton,	1	6	9	Ditto ditto.
E. Connell & sisters,	Urania,	4	18	0½	Sent to the Rev. Mr. McMahon, through Rev. Mr. Sax.
Jas. & Mich. D-nzen,	Columbia,	2	10	0	Ditto ditto.
Ml. Griffin & brothers,	Clarendon,	1	0	0	Ditto ditto.
Pat. & Edw. Syrell,	Syria,	10	1	9½	Rev. B. O'Reilley.
Dennis Courtney,	Agnes,	10	0	0	Rev. B. McGauran.
Dr. John Benson,	Syria,	2	17	6	Ditto ditto.
Dennis Conway,	Sisters,	10	0	0	Ditto, as stated by T. Collin's steward.
Sarah McAveny,	Pursuit,	0	15	0	Rev. Mr. Sax.
Elizabeth Jackson,	Junior,	10	5	6	Rev. B. O'Reilley.
— Cochran,	Ditto,	3	11	0	ditto.
John Morarty,	Sir H. Pottinger,	6	9	6	Rev. Mr. Dogas.
Thomas Murphy,	Odessa,	6	9	6	Rev. T. McDonnell.
William Broderick,	Naparima,	0	10	8¾	Rev. T. B A. Ferland.
Dennis Burns,	John Munn,	6	0	0	Rev. T. McDonnell.
Ann Mylan,	Free Trader,	8	0	0	Ditto ditto.
Richard Meban,	Covenanter,	1	5	0	Rev. B. McGauran.
Theresa Dolly & Marg.,	Bridgeton,	104	10	0	Ditto ditto.
John Kennedy,	Erin's Queen,	2	11	0	Ditto ditto.
James Kernan,	Virginia,	1	2	0	Rev. Mr. Tardif.
George & Mary Cox,	Achilles,	9	4	0	Rev. Mr. Proult.
Catharine Coulan,	Clarendon,	8	0	0	Rt. Revd. Bishop Montreal, forwarded to Mr. Buchanan, Emigrant Agent.
Thad. Reguey,					
James Watson.	Unicorn,	45	0	0	To be sent to his father at Sherbrooke

Name	Ship	£	s	d	Notes
Martin M. Farlane,	Rose,	0	2	0	
Ellen McKay,	Orlando,	0	13	0½	
William Burns,	Progress,	4	9	9½	
George Shane,	Ann,	0	8	9	
Stephen Begrail,	Ditto,	0	9	8	
John Berry,	Free Briton,	0	16	0	
Michael O'Brien,	Tamerac,	0	2	0	
James Gilman,	Agnes,	1	9	0	
Hugh Croib,	Huron,	2	8	0	
James Dwyer,	Wakefield,	0	14	0	
George Bewley,	Goliah,	1	9	0½	
Mary Newling,	Ditto,	0	13	6	
John Regan,	Jessie,	8	0	0	In £1 Notes Son Bantry, County Cork.
Michael Greenock,	Ditto,	0	2	6	And common Silver Watch.
John Boat,	Unicorn,	0	8	6	
Barnard Clark,	Lady Milton,	0	4	6	
Margaret Kelly,	Sarah,	3	16	6	
Andrew Shannon,	Lady F. Hastings,	0	0	2¾	
Mr. Feitrct,	Ditto,	0	9	0	
David Jenkins,	Greenock,	1	5	6	
Ant Penn,	Triton,	0	7	8	
Philip Casey,	Ditto,	8	0	0	And common Silver Watch.
George Kay,	John Jordan,	1	10	2	
Andrew Layton,	Argo,	0	10	4	
James McKay,	Merchs. Aberdeen,	0	8	0	
Martin Sullivan,	Sir H. Pottinger,	1	1	0	
Patrick Sheman,	John & Robert,	1	7	6	
John Irwin,	Ditto,	5	7	0	
Catharine Fraser,	Brown,	129	0	0	Family supposed to be in Canada West.
Alex Mahire,	Ann Kenny,	1	0	0	
Mary A. McKay,	Yorkshire,	0	5	0	
Patrick Carns,	Brown,	8	0	0	
James O'Brian,	Junior,	0	8	0	
Michael O'Donoghue,	Panioras,	4	0	0	
Edward English,	Ditto,	0	1	6	
Joseph Payne,	Aramintn,	1	2	6	
Elizabeth Thompson,	Ditto,	5	17	0	
— Furlough,	Progress,	0	8	0	
Bridget Lenan,	Ditto,	0	3	0	
Thomas Birnic,	Ditto,	0	9	0	
Patrick Walsh,	Royal Adelaide,	6	0	0	Has a Son in County Sligo, care of Father Conway.
Mary Webb,	Avon,	0	5	0	Son living with Mr. Stafford Clasm, lain St. Quebec
Lawrence Gilmore,	X L,	0	2	6	
— Brown,	John Moor,	8	0	0	
Jill Byrne,	John Munn,	8	0	0	
Mary Clancy,	Westmoreland,	0	14	1	Father & Mother in Guernsey.
James Bailie,	Zealous,	2	10	0	
Denis McIartey,	Ellen Simpson,	1	0	0	

Name	Ship	Relative / Address	£ s d	Name	Ship	Relative / Address	£ s d	Disposition
[..] Smith	Yorkshire,		0 5 0	John Brien,	Avon,		$ 0 0 0	To Mr. Buchanan, for orphan children.
Michael Sullivan,	Sir H. Pottinger,	Mother Mary, Tiernatalta Cason, County Kerry.	4 10 0				8 0 0	Ditto ditto.
Edward Qule,	Lotus,		1 0 8¼	Mr. Tracey,	Ann Kenny,	Yorkshire.	60 0 0	Remitted to Emgt. Agent, Kingston, Watch and Gold Ring.
Mary McCarty,	Junior,		0 6 0	Thomas Robinshall,				
William Caveney,	Triton,	{ Mother Mary, Parish of Bullypowel, care of Father Bush.	1 0 0	Robert Tweedy,	Broom,		23 0 0	Remitted to Mr. Buchanan.
William Bryan,	Junior,		0 8 0	Cath. & Ellen Snol,	Lady Campbell,		23 0 0	Ditto ditto.
Mary Creamey,	Lady Campbell,		2 4 0	Donald McDonald,	Ann Runkin,		4 18 0	Given to Dr. Cook, through Mr. Symes.
[..]	Marinus,		0 1 10¼					
Peter Welsh,	Free Trader,		1 6 0	Catherine Bready,	Superior,		2 4 0	Sent to Mr. Buchanan,
Mary Hara,	Lark,		1 0 8	Mary, John & Alice McCabe	Ditto,		2 0 0	Ditto.
Mary Pamujin,	Ganges,		1 12 6	Sarah Hayes,	Jessie,		8 0 0	Ditto.
[..] Cain,	Marinus,		0 4 0	Not known two orphans,			Cy. 0 15 0	Ditto.
Mary Coffee,	Lark,		0 8 0	Cath. & Ellen Wax,*			18 4 0	Ditto.
[..] Burk,	Erin's Queen,	Son Anthony, Toronto, Canada West.	0 8 0	Sarah Taylor,	Westmoreland,		1 0 0	Ditto.
[..] Tooley,	Ellen Simpson,		0 8 0					
							£329 16 6¼	

These remain unclaimed and in Store, 204 Boxes and Trunks; a large number of Feather Beds and great quantity of Wearing Apparel belonging to deceased.

The above amount is all in sterling money, except that of Wax,* which is the proceeds of an Order upon Mr. Wilson, Quebec, and remitted here in currency. The various sums received by the R. C. Clergymen have been for the orphans of the deceased.

(Signed),

MURDOCH McKAY,
Hospital Steward.

h-2

INDEX

Printed by
Marquis, Montmagny, Qc